1001
IMAGES OF
DOGS

CRESCENT BOOKS
NEW YORK • AVENEL, NEW JERSEY

CONTENTS

CLB 2898
© 1992 Colour Library Books Ltd, Godalming, Surrey, England
This 1992 edition published by Crescent Books,
Distributed by Outlet Book Company, Inc., a Random House Company,
40 Engelhard Avenue, Avenel, New Jersey, 07001
Printed and bound in Singapore
ISBN 0 517 06942 3
8 7 6 5 4 3 2 1

INTRODUCTION

A great deal has been written about the dog, for centuries Man's "best friend." However, the origins of this relationship remain an enigma to this day. The dog is an animal which occupies a unique and privileged place in our lives, as friend, helper and protector, and with no other animal has such a relationship ever existed.

This is a book for dog lovers. Though most of us can only own one or two at best, this remarkable new book allows us to enjoy a great number of them: 1,000 pictures of dogs of every conceivable type: pet dogs, solitary dogs, pack dogs, family dogs, big and small dogs, affectionate and aggressive dogs, puppies and old dogs, aristocrats and mongrels; all caught by the camera at a special moment in time.

International in its approach, about a hundred breeds from the major groups are represented here: sheepdogs, house pets, terriers and hounds, hunting dogs, guard dogs and working dogs, including many which you may never have seen before. And, of course, the magnificent dogs which help the handicapped and take care of us are here, too.

Above all this is a picture book to be enjoyed. The concise text is an addition to the main object of the book, in which the pictures tell the story. We leave it to your imagination to interpret them; with a little help from the descriptions, history and anecdotes about each breed.

This book may help you find the dog that is right for you, regardless of its pedigree. Catching a glimpse of the unusual, as well as the more normal lives of the dogs in this book, may well be your introduction to a companion who will enrich your life. Along the way it will provide a lifetime of pleasurable browsing for dog lovers everywhere.

HOUSE PETS

BASENJI • CHIHUAHUA
YORKSHIRE TERRIER
CAVALIER KING CHARLES SPANIEL

The origins of the **Basenji**, which comes from South Africa, go back into antiquity. It is also known as the Congo dog. It was used in Africa for hunting and as a watchdog. It reached the United States in 1941. With its calm, affectionate temperament, it is today best known as a pet dog. An unusual feature of this breed is that it does not bark like other dogs but makes a soft, yodelling call.

The **Chihuahua** has the distinction – and handicap – of being the smallest dog in the world. It was first registered in the United States in 1904, and its name comes from the province of Mexico where it originated. The Aztecs worshipped it and also considered it a delicacy on the table.

Its huge ears and alert eyes give the impression that it is constantly watchful. Never still, it compensates for its small size with a strident voice which it makes sure is always heard – sometimes unnecessarily! Unable to attack larger dogs or other hazards, it has a highly developed sense of danger. Despite its puny appearance, the chihuahua is a robust little dog which has adapted well to all climates. This pocket sized dog is affectionate, faithful and possessive. It hates to be left alone and, intelligent and cunning, it can put on an air of helplessness. Its size destined it to be a lap dog and it lives up to the role magnificently.

The **Yorkshire Terrier**, a comparatively recent breed (1800s), bred in Yorkshire, England, is often seen with a bow in its hair, as owners of "Yorkies" may treat them like dolls. It is now a very fashionable dog, having started life as a rat catcher in a coal mining area. But the "Yorkie" has its moments and, although not an aggressive animal, if attacked it will fight back. This playful and cuddly dog loves children and, like them, can occasionally be temperamental. With correct training it can achieve a high standard of obedience.

The **Cavalier King Charles Spaniel** is a smaller version of the King Charles Spaniel. A lively pet, it can be rather nervous and is a good hunting dog over open country. A very adaptable dog, it is very fond of human company. This breed was first accepted by the American Kennel Club in 1945.

15

12

13

14

Basenji

From 40-42cm (16-18 inches) in height* and from 10-11kg (22-24 pounds) in weight. The coat is short and silky, reddish brown or tan colored with white patches.

Photos: 1, 7 & 10

Chihuahua

They can weigh as little as 1kg (2 pounds 4 ounces), but some reach 2kg (4 pounds 8 ounces). From 15-22cm (5-7 inches) in height. The coat is usually short and straight but there is also a longer, wavy coated variety. They can be reddish brown, silver, black or blue-gray in color.

Photos: 2, 6 (long haired), **8, 13** (short haired) and **15**

Cavalier King Charles

From 25-34cm (10-13 inches) in height and 4.5-8kg (9-17 pounds) in weight. They have a soft, wavy, long coat which can be black and reddish brown in color, all red, white with red patches or all three colors.

Photos: 5, 11 & 12

Yorkshire Terrier

Up to 25cm (10 inches) in height and 3.5kg (7 1/2 pounds) in weight. They have a long, sily coat, very full on the head. Their coat is two-colored; steely-blue to the base of the tail and red on the chest.

Photos: 3, 4, 9, 14

The measurements given in this book refer to height at the shoulder. The lower figure given is for the smallest female dogs and the higher figure for the largest male dogs.

DALMATIAN • JAPANESE SPITZ
FRENCH BULLDOG
ENGLISH BULLDOG
FRENCH POODLE

The **Dalmatian** does not come from Dalmatia and is certainly not of Yugoslavian origin, despite its name. Made popular in recent times by the Disney film, *101 Dalmatians,* varying ideas as to its origins abound. One theory is that it may have come from Asia to England in the 18th century via Egypt and Greece. It is a dog of many skills and was used for carrying messages in the Balkan wars. It makes a good watchdog, sheepdog, sled dog, and, in some countries, has even been used as a seeing-eye dog for the blind. The Dalmatian is very popular in the United States as the fire house mascot, often riding in the fire engines when they are called out. It is often pictured wearing a fire helmet, and "Sparky" is a popular name. It is a dog with a calm temperament which enjoys playing with children. The Dalmatian has a slightly melancholy air and depends, even more than most dogs, on human companionship. Its white coat with black or brown spots is internationally recognizable. It is a strange fact that Dalmatian puppies are born with plain white coats.

The **Japanese Spitz** has slanting eyes and, like all Spitzes, it makes a remarkable pet. Its charm and the pure white of its coat make it a dog sought after for its appearance, as well as for its intelligence, playfulness and affectionate nature.

The **Bulldog** was developed centuries ago (in the 1200s) in Great Britain and was used for bull baiting. The modern bulldog has had the ferocity bred out of it and it is typically gentle and reliable. It has a large head, folded ears and short muzzle with a protruding jaw, and loose skin that forms wrinkles on its head and face. An affectionate family pet, it is grouped in the non-sporting dogs group of the American Kennel Club.

The **French Bulldog,** as its name suggests, is a native of France. After much cross breeding it has become a rather small dog with the characteristics of a mastiff: large head and sullen look. American breeders have preserved the "bat ear" which is a distinctive feature of the breed. Today, it has nothing in common with the more ferocious breeds of bulldog. A big dog with short legs, it makes a good and affectionate family pet.

The **Poodle** has disputed origins; some say it was first bred in France, some in Denmark, Germany or Italy. It certainly became so popular in France that it is now the

national dog of that country and is often known as the French Poodle. It comes in three types: the Standard, Miniature and Toy poodle, all of which were first registered in the United States, where they are very popular, in 1887. A faithful companion and an elegant animal, often pampered, it always seems happy and ready to play. It makes a clever circus dog, and has been used for hunting as well as being a popular model for the great Renaissance and 18th century artists. Reputed to be one of the most intelligent dogs, the Poodle makes a fun, lively pet with a particularly well developed sense of smell.

Dalmatian
From 55-60cm (21-23 inches) in height. Weight should be around 25kg (55 pounds). They should have as many, clearly separated, black or reddish brown spots as possible.
Photos: 1, 8 & 12

Japanese Spitz
Height varies from 25-40cm (10-15 inches) The fur is straight, long and thick, and the coat is completely white.
Photo: 2

Bulldog
From 30-35cm (11-14 inches) in height and weight should be 22-30kg (48-66 pounds). The coat is very short and thick, fawn or white in color or fawn with white patches.
Photos: 6, 9 & 11.

French Bulldog
From 8-14kg (17-30 pounds) in weight. The coat is short and shiny, brindle or white with black patches.
Photos: 4, 5, 7 & 14

French Poodle
Standard: from 46-55cm (17-22 inches) in height; Miniature: from 36-45cm (13-15 inches); Toy: 25cm (10 inches) and under. Weight varies between 20kg (44 pounds) for a big Standard dog and 6kg (13 pound) for a small toy female. The coat is curly and may be chocolate, black, champagne or gray.
Photos: 3, 10, 13 & 15

TIBETAN SPANIEL • PUG
CHOW CHOW • SHAR-PEI

The **Tibetan Spaniel** is probably related to the Pekingese and the Pug. It has a feathery tail and ears that hang down, but really nothing else in common with any other type of spaniel. It makes a good pet but can be shy and wary of strangers. It is as happy with city life as it is living in the country.

The **Pug** was first registered with the American Kennel Club in 1885. It has all the fascination of a big dog – in miniature. Its square muzzle and round head, with much-wrinkled forehead, make it look both fierce and touching. Despite its very black muzzle, flattened nose and awkward body, it is a dog that has charmed many with its gentle, affectionate nature. It can, however, be aggressive with strangers. A dog much favored in high society in the eighteenth and nineteenth centuries, it appears in many famous paintings.

The **Chow Chow** comes from the same family as the Spitz, and resembles other sled dogs, such as the Alaskan Malemute. Slightly slanting eyes, face buried in a mass of thick fur out of which stick only the pointed ears and the end of a flattened nose, it presents to the world a scowling, uncommunicative appearance. Rather lazy, it usually only does what its owner says and can be very ferocious if approached by someone it does not know. Its introversion may be due to its background. Chow Chows were used to pull carts in 18th century China, where they were also eaten with much enjoyment by emperor and peasant alike. They love rice, which they sometimes even prefer to meat.

The **Shar-Pei**, once a Chinese fighting dog, has become one of the gentlest of pets. With its sad, baggy eyes and heavy folds of loose skin, it is unusual and enchanting. Some people think it is just wrinkly and ugly, but all agree that it is unique. The blue Shar-Pei is one of the most sought-after colors. In 1971 only a few specimens of this breed were known to exist, but it is now making a comeback in the United States.

7

12

8

9

13

16

10

14

11

15

Tibetan Spaniel

Size is around 25cm (10 inches) in height and weight about 6.5kg (14 pounds). The flat coat is thick and may be white, fawn, any shade of brown, or black.

Photos: 6, 8 & 13

Pug

Very muscular, they should not weigh more than 8kg (17 pounds). The coat is flat and shiny and is usually cream, a warm tan, silver or black.

Photos: 2, 7 & 14

Chow Chow

From 46-60cm (18-23 inches) in height and 18-25kg (39-55 pounds) in weight. Always single colored, usually fawn, they may also be blue, cream, black or silver.

Photos: 4, 9, 10, 12 & 15

Shar-Pei

A compact-looking dog. Medium sized, between 40 and 50cm (15-19 inches) in height and 16-25kg (35-55 pounds) in weight. The coat is short and dense, fawn, cream or blue colored.

Photos: 1, 3, 5, 11 (blue Shar-Pei) & 16

CHINESE HAIRLESS DOG
SPITZ • SHIBA-INU
GRIFFON BELGE

Despite its name, the origins of the **Chinese Hairless Dog** are uncertain, but it may have come from Africa. Despite its apparently slight build, it is actually quite a robust little dog. As the name suggests, it has no hair on its body. The only hair it has grows in comical tufts on the top of its head and sometimes on its face, feet and the end of its tail. Nevertheless it possesses a certain charm, and it is a proud and elegant dog. The shape of its head and ears and its dark colored nose add to its strange appearance. Delicate and needing a lot of care, it is sensitive and affectionate and gets on well with children, making it a very good pet.

The origin of the **Spitz** is a matter for argument; some say it is German, some Dutch and some Russian. Like all dogs of the same family, this breed is closely related to the first dogs to be domesticated. There is evidence that it existed in ancient Egypt. It was used for many different purposes and was once the favorite companion of Dutch bargemen. An alert expression, triangular ears and a plumed tail characterize the Spitz. Friendly and adaptable, it will even guard sheep, though it is not classed as a sheepdog. As a house dog it has no equal, both as a pet and guardian of its home and family. The eating habits of the Spitz can be hard on the pocket; it is best to accustom it early on to a diet that is not too concentrated on meat!

The **Shiba-Inu** is a Japanese dog. Related to the Chow Chow it is an ancient breed of the Spitz family. A dog of varied talents, it makes a good watchdog, pet and, occasionally, hunter of small animals.

The **Griffon Belge** was first registered in the United States in 1910. It is a fun mixture: part Schnauzer, part Pug, part terrier. A small pet dog which often looks bad tempered but is usually gentle, obedient and affectionate, its Gremlin-like appearance attracts sympathy, but beware, it can be difficult with small children.

8

13

9

11

14

10

Chinese Hairless Dog

From 40-50cm (15-20 inches) in height. Its skin is usually gray with reddish patches on the chest.
Photos: 1, 3, 6, 8, 10 & 13

Spitz

From 45-60cm (17-24 inches) in height. May weigh as much as 20kg (44 pounds). The coat is thick all over the body and there are four colors of Spitz: silver gray, black, pure white and tan.
Photos: 4, 12 & 14

Shiba-Inu

From 35-41cm (14-16 inches) in height. It has a thick, dense coat which may be red, gray and white (speckled or brindle), white or slate colored.
Photo: 5

Griffon Belge

There is no standard size for the Griffon. Weight may vary from 3-5kg (6-11 pounds). The coat is tough and luxuriant and may be black, black and red or black and tan.
Photos: 2, 7, 9 (long haired) & 11

12

SHI-TZU • MALTESE TERRIER BICHON HAVANAIS COTON DE TULEAR

The **Shi-Tzu** bears a Chinese name, which means "lion." This dog was given more veneration by the Chinese than they accorded to a real lion. It was not seen in Europe until around the 1930s, and it reached the zenith of its popularity in the '50s. It was first registered by the American Kennel Club in 1969. It strongly resembles the Lhasa Apso in the shape of its body and the Pekingese in the shape of its nose. It is a home-loving dog that likes its creature comforts, but it is also full of fun and energy.

Despite its name the **Maltese Terrier,** according to some experts, does not come from the Mediterranean island of Malta but from much further east; Asia in fact. The Italians call it the Melita after an Adriatic Island of that name. All are agreed, however, that it is one of the most ancient breeds: a watchdog in ancient Egypt, a family pet for the rich Athenians of classical Greece, and a well known figure at the French court of Louis XV. The pure white of its coat and the silky texture of its fur give it a quality image: that of a luxury dog, usually owned by ladies. Women love to make a lap dog of the Maltese Terrier, dressing its hair with little red bows. A sweet and gentle dog, not the least bit aggressive, it is gifted with exceptional hearing which puts it on the alert at the tiniest sound.

The **Bichon Havanais** is of even more uncertain origins. Maltese-Cuban perhaps? From the Antilles? Or a bit of all of these? Whichever, it is a rare and enchanting pet.

The **Coton de Tuléar** comes from Madagascar. Very similar to the Maltese terrier in appearance, it is a great companion and a good swimmer and walker.

Shi-Tzu

Maximum size is just over 25cm (10 inches) and it should not weigh more than 8kg (17 pounds).The coat is long, thick and slightly wavy. A variety of colors are accepted.
Photos: 1, 3, 4, 8, 10 & 12

Maltese Terrier

Maximum size is 25cm (10 inches) and weight varies between 3 and 4kg (6 and 9 pounds). The coat is long, silky and straight with a long strip in the center of the forehead. A long-lived dog: 18 years is not an unusual age for a Maltese Terrier.
Photos: 7 & 11

Bichon Havanais

Size is around 25cm (10 inches) in height and weight about 6kg (13 pounds). The coat is long, soft and wavy. White or fawn colored, gray or white and fawn.
Photos 6 & 9

Coton de Tuléar

From 28-31cm (11-13 inches) in height and 3.5-4kg (8-9 pounds) in weight. The coat is long and luxuriant, resembling cotton in texture, hence its name. Always pure white.
Photos: 2, 5, 13 & 14

WELSH CORGI • DACHSHUND

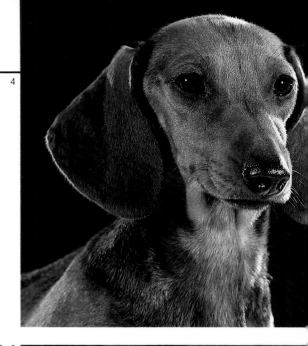

The **Welsh Corgi** comes, of course, from Wales. It is normally grouped in the sheepdog class, being used for herding sheep from the Middle Ages onward and for hunting before that. But its appearance and small size make it look to the average person as though it should belong to the Basset group. Famous as a pet in the British royal family, it is the Queen's favorite breed. The Corgi is a good sheepdog, watchdog and companion. There are two kinds of Corgis: the Pembroke and the Cardigan, the latter long tailed and rough coated. The Pembroke has practically no tail. Both types are affectionate, calm, energetic and intelligent.

The **Dachshund** probably belongs to the same family as the Basset Hound. A German dog of ancient origins, it can be seen on Egyptian bas-reliefs. There are three types of Dachshund of distinctly differing size and coat: long haired, smooth haired and wire haired. Its size might suggest that the Dachshund is a lap dog, but in fact it is an excellent terrier, once used for badger hunting. It is generally thought of as a pet which is nervous, restless, obstinate, liking its own way, temperamental and jealous. None of which stops its owners from being besotted by it or letting their lives be taken over by the dog! The Dachshund has no equal when it comes to getting around people.

8

13

9

10

14

Welsh Corgi

From 25-30cm (10-12 inches) in height and 8-12kg (17-26 pounds) in weight. The coat of the Cardigan Corgi is short and rougher than the Pembroke's, which is medium long and soft. They may be one colored, red, fawn, tan or black or with white markings.
Photos: 1, 6, 8,12 & 16

Dachshund

Depending on type the size varies from 12-22cm (5-9 inches) in height. Weight varies from 9kg (18 pounds) for the Standard Dachshund to 4kg (9 pounds) for the Medium Dachshund and 3.5kg (8 pounds) for the Miniature. The coat is red or bi-colored: black and brown or silver with white markings. An all white, or all black, coat is considered a fault.
Photos: 2, 3, 4, 10, 11 & 14 (short haired), **7, 9 & 15** (long haired), **5 & 13** (rough coated).

11

15

16

12

LHASA APSO
MINIATURE PINSCHER
AUSTRIAN PINSCHER
GERMAN PINSCHER • PEKINGESE

The **Lhasa Apso**, which comes from Tibet, is a curious cross between a Terrier and a Tibetan Spaniel. It takes its name from the town of Lhasa, where it lived in the monasteries. Once considered sacred, today the Lhasa Apso is merely a family pet, but one whose acute hearing makes it a good watchdog.

The **Miniature Pinscher** comes from the Pinscher family, which is itself a subtle cross of Schnauzer, Doberman and Manchester Terrier. A highly popular dog in the United States, where the Miniature Pinscher Club of America was formed in 1929. It is only a little bigger than a Chihuahua, with a sharp muzzle, very black nose and pointed ears. Being related to the terrier family it makes a good rat catcher. Robust, obedient, and no trouble to look after, it makes an ideal pet.

The **Austrian Pinscher**, despite its name, should not be confused with either the Standard or Miniature Pinscher. Although an excellent watchdog, it is first and foremost a good pet. Small and full of energy it can also be aggressive, although it is a calm dog generally and, being good with children, it makes a suitable family dog.

The **German Pinscher** is from an ancient line. Although inclined to bark stridently at strangers, it is not a vicious dog. But its bark is certainly disturbing! It combines the qualities of a good watchdog and pet.

The **Pekingese** is an ancient Chinese breed, which could once be owned only by Emperors. It inhabited the Forbidden City for 16 centuries. Maybe its sacred antecedents have given the Pekingese the slightly condescending air of nobility which the it displays today. A luxury loving dog, it likes silky cushions and the fluffy slippers of its mistress and is definitely a woman's dog. One of the most ancient breeds in the world, it is not very interested in outdoor pursuits but loves its home and its owners for whom, alone, it reserves its attention.

Lhasa Apso

From 20-25cm (8-10 inches) in height and 5-7kg (11-15 pounds) in weight, its coat is abundant and the fur falls over its eyes. Color may be sable, slate, brindle, black or white or a combination of these.

Photos: 1, 2, 10 & 13

Miniature Pinscher

Size is about 30cm (11 inches) high. The coat is short, smooth and shiny, often black in color with red markings.

Photos: 3, 7 & 9

Austrian Pinscher

Size is about 50cm (20 inches) high and weight around 18kg (40 pounds). Short haired, its coat is sandy, black or brindle with white markings.

Photos: 4 & 5

German Pinscher

From 45-48cm (17-19 inches) in height and around 16kg (35 pounds) in weight. Its short haired coat is similar in color to that of the Doberman: black, black and red, chocolate, brown and blue/gray.

Photo: 11

Pekingese

15-25cm (6-10 inches) high, its weight varies between 2 and 8kg (4 and 16 pounds). It has a short, flat, black nose The coat is luxuriant and tough, with long skirts, and may be any color except white.

Photos: 6, 8 & 12

SHEEPDOGS

BRIARD · ROUGH COLLIE

The French **Briard** is, today, well known outside the country of its origin, as well as being popular in France. An ancient breed, mention of it is found in French Medieval treatises on hunting, and it figures in 15th-century Italian primitive art. Its slightly rough appearance, agility and amazing liveliness make it a dog of contrasting character: a good sheepdog and a fun companion. It is also the "James Bond" of the dog world, having been used to carry messages behind enemy lines and as a Red Cross dog in the First World War. It is also used as a seeing-eye dog for the blind and as a mountain rescue dog. Intelligent, affectionate and particularly attached to its owner, it makes a great family dog, being very good with children and particularly vigilant on their behalf.

The **Rough Collie** is probably the result of a number of crosses between sheepdogs and greyhounds. A splendid dog of great charm, the breed has been immortalized in the character of *Lassie,* the archetypal collie, with her sandy and white coat, long ruff and flowing mane of hair. Gentle and sensitive, the Collie can look heartbreakingly sad. It is the perfect pet, particularly for people on their own or where there are children. Resistant to wet and cold, it does not like the heat and is happiest in the wide open spaces.

Briard

From 56-68cm (21-27 inches) in height and 20-30kg (45-65 pounds) in weight. The coat is spectacular: long, thick, slightly wavy and heavy. Black, fawn or gray, they are always one colored.

Photos: 2, 4, 5, 6, 9, 13, 14 & 15

Rough Collie

Size varies from 51-61cm (20-24 inches) in height and weight from 18-29kg (40-64 pounds). The coat is very thick with a luxuriant mane and ruff.

Photos: 1, 3, 7, 8, 10, 11, 12 & 16

BOUVIER DES FLANDRES MAREMANER PYRENEAN SHEEPDOG

The **Bouvier des Flandres,** with its forbidding and slightly unprepossessing air, is a really efficient animal. A good watchdog, ski patrol dog, and used by the police and the army, it is also suitable for looking after cattle or pulling a sled. Its sense of smell, its intelligence and strength endear it to many different kinds of owner. Despite its unprepossessing appearance (tousled coat and thick eyelids) it is a gentle, calm, loyal animal and makes one of the best family pets. But it can be a redoubtable watchdog; beware of touching anything or anyone dear to the Bouvier!

The **Maremaner,** or Abruzzian Sheepdog, is one of the oldest sheepdog breeds. Pure white, it has an alert and intelligent eye. Running well over difficult terrain, its aim in life is to be a good working sheepdog. No sheep gets away from the Maremaner and it is particularly vigilant of enemies of its flock – human or animal. Used to high mountain pastures and the wide open spaces it hates to be shut in, but its easy temperament and adaptability make it a great pet, provided it is given enough exercise. Robust and resistant to illness, it will adapt to any diet but never says no to a meal of meat!

The **Pyrenean Sheepdog** (not to be confused with the Pyrenean Mountain Dog from which it is descended) is the veteran breed of French sheepdogs. There are three kinds: the long haired (best known), the medium long haired and the smooth faced, long nosed. Totally at home in the mountains, where it is the shepherd's right hand, it is intelligent, bossy and sometimes nervous. It knows how to make itself respected by other animals, including horses, and its acute sense of hearing makes it an excellent watchdog. Much attached to its owner, and loving children, it makes a trustworthy pet.

Bouvier des Flandres

Impressively large, it stands from 59-68cm (23-29 inches) high. Weight can be as much as 40kg (88 pounds). The coat is very dense and rough haired and it has a luxuriant moustache and beard.

Photos: 4, 9, 11 & 14

Maremaner

A big dog, 65-73cm (25-28 inches) in height and weighing from 30-40kg (66 to 88 pounds). The coat is white, straight and long haired.

Photos: 1, 3, 7, 10 & 12

Pyrenean Sheepdog

From 38-48cm (15-18 inches) in height and weighing 8-15kg (17-33 pounds). The coat may be long haired, medium long haired, smooth or wavy. The fur does not cover the eyes. The coat is usually light brown in color.

Photos: 2, 5, 6, 8, 13 & 15

PICARDY SHEEPDOG
HUNGARIAN KOMONDOR
GROENENDAEL

O ne of the oldest European sheepdog breeds, the **Picardy Sheepdog** was probably introduced to Europe by invading Celts, some centuries B.C. Nearly extinct by the 1940s, the breed survived despite being forgotten by the showing world. Its characteristics include pointed ears, alert expression and a soft heart. An efficient sheepdog it, is completely unaggressive and is perfect with children.

The **Hungarian Komondor** is unlike any other dog, with its thick, corded coat resembling the wool on a sheep. Its muzzle is completely hidden, giving it a mysterious look. Hardy, faithful and courageous, it never balks at the task of herding sheep, and is a watchdog to be respected; not even afraid of wolves, which its ancestors often encountered. It is used to working at night and resting during the day. Its habit of attacking silently is particularly spine chilling and this is a dog which inspires respect and even fear as well as affection. It can be very gentle with children and is a sensitive dog, occasionally sulking behind its cloak of hair! A good pet but it does need a lot of exercise and fresh air and should not be kept in an apartment. Molting heavily, its fur will tangle quickly if not brushed every day.

The **Groenendael,** or Belgian Sheepdog, is a cousin of the German Shepherd, easily distinguished from it by its shiny black coat. An attractively elegant animal, it has been a member of the Belgian and French courts since the Middle Ages, and as a dog of many facets, it is only a question of choosing the job you need it to do: herding sheep, guarding the home or working as a mountain rescue dog. Very attached to its owner, the Groenendael adores children and is difficult to resettle if it changes homes. But it can be capricious and bad tempered and is best approached with care by strangers.

Picardy Sheepdog

From 55-65cm (22-25 inches) in height. Medium long haired, its coat is straight and completely waterproof: not a single drop of water filters through to the skin.

Photos: 1, 3, 8 & 14

Hungarian Komondor

Size is around 80cm (31 inches) high for a male dog and 70cm (27 inches) for a female. Weight varies from 40-60kg (88-132 pounds). The eyes are dark brown and the coat a whitish gray.

Photos: 2, 4, 6, 12 & 13

Groenendael

From 58-62cm (23-24 inches) in height. Ideal weight is around 28kg (60 pounds). Sometimes they have a white blaze on the chest. This is not a fault but is said to be a mark of their noble ancestry, handed down from the "Duke of Groenendael."

Photos: 5, 7, 9, 10 & 11

BORDER COLLIE
CATALAN SHEEPDOG
OVCHARKA

The **Border Collie** is one of the greatest dogs for herding sheep. Endowed with an extraordinary sense of smell and an ability to concentrate its gaze unflinchingly (to the extent of being able to hypnotize the sheep), its deepest instinct is to herd. It is therefore very unhappy if kept in an apartment or living an inactive life. This breed, which originated in Scotland, works untiringly and with total dedication to the job. It is also a sensitive and loving dog much attached to its owner, whose orders it will obey to the letter.

The **Catalan Sheepdog** is related to the Pyrenean Sheepdog, with the same pointed ears, thick coat and smiling, expressive eyes. This hairy, attractively untidy dog is a tireless guardian of its flocks as well as being able to perform other tasks: security work, police work, carrying messages and so on. It can learn any task and bravely carry it out. Obedient and docile it loves the company of humans, making it an excellent pet.

The **Ovcharka** is from southern Russia and is descended from the giant Russian hounds. A rare, enormous breed, its forbidding air makes it a great watchdog.

Border Collie

Size for the standard is around 53cm (21 inches) high and weight about 20kg (44 pounds). The coat may be straight and long or smooth and short but should always be short on the head and paws.
Photos: 1, 4, 6, 8 & 14

Catalan Sheepdog

There is no American Kennel Club standard for the Catalan Sheepdog. The coat may be long or short and wavy. Usually gray and white, sometimes with tawny markings.
Photos: 2, 5, 7, 10 & 13

Ovcharka

Can be as much as 80cm (32 inches) high and weigh as much as 50kg (110 pounds)! A very hairy coat: off white or gray in color.
Photos: 3, 9, 11 & 12

ANATOLIAN SHEPHERD DOG
OLD ENGLISH SHEEPDOG
BERNESE MOUNTAIN DOG

The **Anatolian Shepherd Dog** is, as it names suggests, a native of Anatolia in Turkey. Its appearance is curiously untypical of a sheepdog, being smooth and short coated, light in color, with a black nose and ears. This ancient breed is known as the "Turkish guard dog." Fighting, hunting, protecting; they all come naturally to this breed, which carries out its work conscientiously. Dangerous to strangers, its size alone makes it extremely effective as a guard dog, but to its own family it is gentle and affectionate and good with children.

The **Old English Sheepdog** is a breed descended, probably, from Italian sheepdogs imported into England by the Romans. Today it is the most typically British dog; famous in England for many years now as the star of paint commercials, which have done much to popularize it. Much valued as a sheepdog in the days when it was used mainly in that role, it is now a favorite family pet. It is still capable of herding together stray children when out on a walk! An extremely exuberant dog, it needs firm obedience training to be manageable and lots of exercise to tire it out. Neither by temperament nor size is it suited to a living room existence.

The **Bernese Mountain Dog** comes from Switzerland, where it is nicknamed "the bear." One of four varieties of Swiss mountain dog, it was introduced into that country more than 2,000 years ago by Roman soldiers. Wary of strangers but much attached to its owners, this is a handsome, energetic and intelligent dog. One of the best working sheepdogs.

11

8

12

15

9

13

10

14

Anatolian Shepherd Dog

Can reach as much as 98cm (38 inches) in height and weigh 68kg (150 pounds). The coat is straight and smooth and light colored; cream or light fawn.

Photos: 1, 2, 12 & 15

Old English Sheepdog

From 56-58cm (22-23 inches) in height and 25-30kg (55-66 pounds) in weight. The coat is long, rough and sightly wavy. Gray or gray/blue with white patches.

Photos: 4, 5, 7, 10 & 14

Bernese Mountain Dog

Height: 58-70cm (23-28 inches). Weight: 35-40kg (77-88 pounds). The coat is thick, soft and wavy, black and white or red and white.

Photos: 3, 6, 8, 9, 11 & 13

KUVASZ • BEARDED COLLIE APPENZELL

The **Kuvasz** is a Hungarian breed, established there in the 13th century, and the name derives from a Hungarian word meaning "trustworthy guardian." It is possible that its earliest origins may also have been Mongol, Tibetan or Turk and, as it bears a strong resemblance to the Pyrenean Mountain Dog and the Maremaner, it is difficult to trace its ancestry precisely. An adaptable dog, it is equally at home in the princely surroundings of a Magyar court or running in some great open pasture. Its gentle temperament and handsome appearance make it a wonderful pet.

The **Bearded Collie**, related to the Rough Collie and the Old English Sheepdog, was bred to herd sheep. Its acute sense of smell, its initiative and intelligence have made it an exceptional sheepdog, and its gentle, affectionate nature makes it the perfect pet for children. One of the best known British breeds, it has been around in Britain since the Roman invasion and was probably brought to England at that time. Today this lovely dog is internationally renowned and is as much sought after for its skills as a sheepdog as for its qualities as a pet.

The **Appenzell,** or Alpine Shepherd Dog, comes from Switzerland. A dog of many talents, in addition to being an excellent working sheepdog it is also used as a ski patrol dog, security dog and rescue dog. Not large by comparison with some other Swiss breeds, it is energetic, tireless and hates a sedentary life.

7

11

8

12

Kuvasz

Around 75cm (29 inches) high, weight is about 50kg (110 pounds). Medium long haired, the coat is wavy, thick and tough and is white or cream in color.

Photos: 2, 9, 11 & 13

Bearded Collie

From 55-60cm (21-24 inches) in height and 20-30kg (44-66 pounds) in weight. The coat is long, thick, wavy and tough. Colors go from shades of fawn and gray through black with white markings.

Photos: 3, 4, 5, 10, 12 & 14

Appenzell

From 48-58 cm (19-23 inches) in height and 22-25kg (48-55 pounds) in weight. The coat is short, thick and shiny, fawn or white in color.

Photos: 1, 6, 7, 8 & 15

9

13

14

10

15

33

HOUNDS

SALUKI • SLOUGHI
PHAROAH HOUND • WHIPPET

The **Saluki,** or Persian Hound, comes from Iran, of Asian forebears. It was probably imported from Asia by the Greeks and then by the Romans to the countries they conquered. The Saluki is the dog seen languidly stretched out on an Oriental rug in illustrations from *The Arabian Nights.* Privileged companion of Arab sheikhs, the Saluki is a dog traditionally treated with great respect; for instance, in Arab countries it is not bought and sold but offered as a gift, intended to bestow honor on the recipient. As successful at hunting as it is beautiful, this is one of the most magnificent examples of the hound group.

The **Sloughi,** or Arabian Hound, comes from North Africa. A slim, muscular dog, it is elegant with a royal bearing. Light colored and bony, it can camouflage itself in desert surroundings and was once used to hunt gazelle in the desert. Today Nomad tribes still use it for hunting and as a watchdog. In Europe it is regarded as a much appreciated pet, despite its independent nature. It is not yet recognized by the American Kennel Club.

The **Pharaoh Hound** now comes from Spain and was probably originally imported into that country by the Moors. It is well known in Europe and to a lesser extent in the United States. A good dog for game hunting, and an excellent pet, being playful, gentle and affectionate and not difficult to look after.

The **Whippet,** together with the Italian Greyhound, is the smallest of the hound group and is like a miniature Greyhound. An English breed, it has all the best qualities of the hound: elegance, neatness, speed and an aristocratic air, without any of the disadvantages, such as the group's tendency to fragility and reputation for being difficult. Wonderfully fast, the Whippet can run at speeds up to 30 miles an hour. Like many hounds it is a popular racing dog. Despite its slender build, it is a robust, fit dog; easy to look after, playful and responsive. The perfect pet as long as it gets the fresh air and exercise it needs.

Saluki

From 58-71cm (22-28 inches) tall and 14-25kg (30-55 pounds) in weight. The coat is smooth, soft and silky and longest on the ears and tail. Fawn, gray, cream, black or red in color.
Photos: 1, 2, 5, 7, 8 & 9

Sloughi

From 55-75cm (21-29 inches) in height and 30-40kg (66-88 pounds) in weight. The coat is fine and short haired and usually sandy colored, although other colors do occur: brindle, fawn and black, for example.
Photos: 4, 6, 13 & 15

Pharaoh Hound

From 62-70cm (24-27 inches) in height and there is no standard weight. The coat is close cropped and shining and is reddish brown in color or reddish brown with white markings.
Photos: 3 & 14

Whippet

From 43-49cm (17-19 inches) in height. Weight is around 10kg (22 pounds). The coat is fine and short haired and often slate gray in color. Black, fawn, white, or any of these with white markings, are also accepted.
Photos: 10, 11, 12, 16 & 17

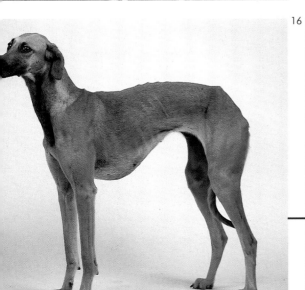

AFGHAN HOUND
ITALIAN GREYHOUND
HUNGARIAN GREYHOUND

The **Afghan** is grouped everywhere in the world in the hound class. It arrived in the United States around 1926, via Britain. The breed originated in the Middle East and is a very ancient one, only introduced into Europe in the 19th century. The breed started as a hunting dog (hunting wolves and jackals) but has now become one of the most sought after (and expensive) pets. Although it may look like "a Greyhound in pajamas," the Afghan is not a slippers and fireside dog. It loves to run and tire itself out and has not forgotten that it was bred to hunt.

The **Italian Greyhound** is the smallest of the true greyhounds. Slender and elegant, despite its small size it has all the Greyhound qualities, including speed. First registered in the United States in 1886, it probably dates back to Roman times or earlier; it is certainly of very ancient origin. Its elegant outline is often seen in the paintings of Italian and other masters. It has a sweet temperament, gentle and affectionate, and can be slightly nervous. It is deeply attached to those who give it affection.

The **Hungarian Greyhound** is short coated and not unlike the Italian Greyhound and the Whippet, but in its veins runs the blood of the true English Greyhound. It comes in the class of hounds known as scent hounds, and is not yet registered with the American Kennel Club. Quiet and affectionate, the Hungarian Greyhound is never "temperamental."

Afghan Hound

From 63-74cm (25-28 inches) in height; weight is around 29kg (64 pounds). Yellow is the most common color but black and white dogs are equally acceptable.
Photos: 1, 2, 4, 7, 9, 10, 13 & 15

Italian Greyhound

Maximum height is 35cm (14 inches) and weight should be under 5kg (11 pounds). The coat is fine, soft and short haired and must be one color: light or dark gray, black or light fawn.
Photos: 3, 6, 10, 12 & 16

Hungarian Greyhound

Height is from 65-70cm (25-27 inches) and weight 22-30kg (48-66 pounds). The coat is short and it may be one color or a mixture of many colors.
Photos: 5, 8, 11 & 14

BORZOI • GALGO ESPAGNOL
IRISH WOLFHOUND

The **Borzoi,** or Russian Wolfhound, is the aristocrat of hounds. This thoroughbred is the epitome of the noble dog. In the last century the Borzoi was a favorite with the Russian Czars and many of the crowned heads of Europe. Companion to the Russian Imperial Family, it was also used for hunting bear. Its origins go back a long way and its haughty look, long nose and air of serenity give it an almost disdainful air. It was first brought to the United States in 1889. Nowadays it is more of a pet dog than a hunter, but one that needs supervised walks, as its romping around can get out of hand! It needs plenty of exercise. Totally at home in the most fashionable surroundings, its calm, reserved temperament, together with its beautiful appearance, make it a pet that is hard to equal.

The **Galgo Espagnol**, or Spanish Wolfhound, is half way between an English Greyhound and an Arabian Hound. The Galgo is still used in Spain for hare coursing, as well as for herding and racing. It is not yet registered with the American Kennel Club. Like all hounds, it is an aristocratic dog but it is also a courageous hunter, not content simply to sit around and look decorative.

The **Irish Wolfhound** is the largest of all the hounds and can grow to 39 inches in height at the shoulder! It is not, however, as aristocratic looking as some other members of the Wolfhound group. Shaggier and rougher in appearance, its wolf hunting origins are immediately apparent and it looks like a dog that could hunt stag or other large predators, as it does in certain countries, including the United States. A quiet, calm, faithful dog with none of the characteristics of the watchdog, despite its tough appearance. But it is not a nervous or lazy dog and needs to tire itself out with fresh air and exercise.

6

11

7

12

16

8

13

9

14

10

15

Borzoi

From 66-80cm (26-31 inches) in height and weight should not exceed 45kg (99 pounds). The coat is soft, silky and wavy. White, black and white with reddish patches, fawn or gold in color.

Photos: 1, 3, 5, 6, 7, 8, 9 & 10

Galgo Espagnol

From 60-70cm (23-27 inches) in height. Weight is 25-30kg (55-66 pounds). The coat is short and relatively coarse in texture; sandy, fawn or orange in color.

Photos: 2, 11, 13 & 15

Irish Wolfhound

The standard is from 70-90cm (27-36 inches) in height and 40-54kg (88-118 pounds) in weight. The coat is short, rough haired and slightly tousled. Gray, black, white and other colors are permitted.

Photos: 4, 12, 14 & 16

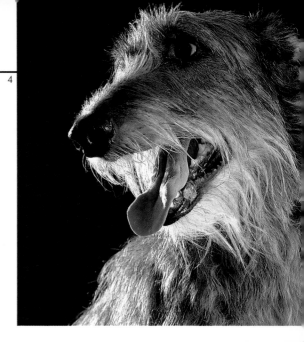

GREYHOUND • DEERHOUND AZAWAKH • IBIZAN HOUND

The English **Greyhound** is the perfect hound, synonymous with all that is elegant and noble in the dog, in which the best qualities of the hound group are found. An English breed, known in the British Isles since ancient times, it is probably related to Eastern breeds, perhaps Greek (its name may be a contraction of Greek Hound). It is the dog of sumptuous royal hunts and the courts of the Middle Ages. The Greyhound is also a great racing dog, capable of running 600 yards in 30 seconds. Used to chase an electric hare at dog racing tracks, it is also still used for coursing in Great Britain. Its ability to run fast over long distances (and its enjoyment of such exercise) does not make it the ideal apartment dog, but it is a great pet if kept in sensible surroundings.

The **Deerhound**, a Scottish breed, is a rather more slender cousin of the Irish Wolfhound, and looks, with its immense and hairy appearance, like a rougher, country relative of the elegant Borzois or Afghans. Once an intrepid hunter of stag (hence its name), today it is a gentle and affectionate pet.

The **Azawakh** is a hound that has only been known in Europe since the 1960s and is not known in the United States. Common among nomad tribes, particularly the Tuareg, it is a type of Sloughi.

The **Ibizan Hound** is a native of the island of Ibiza and is, therefore, a Spanish dog. It is of the Greyhound type but is not, strictly speaking, classified as such. It has, however, many of that breed's qualities, including elegance, speed and hunting skills. It is particularly good at hunting rabbits, with a natural sense of smell which has been cultivated over the years. An instinctive hunter, it also makes a good retriever and scent hound for small prey and can run very fast. It doesn't have the easiest of temperaments and may be aggressive with strangers.

Greyhound

From 76-78cm (29-31 inches) in height. Weight is around 30kg (65 pounds). The coat is smooth and fine and may be black, blue, brindle or gray, with or without white markings.
Photos: 1, 5 & 16

Deerhound

From 71-76cm (27-30 inches) in height. Weight varies from 30-48kg (48-105 pounds). The coat is rough, gray/blue, sandy or fawn in color.
Photos: 2, 4, 7 & 12

Azawakh

There is no standard size and weight for this dog. The coat may be sandy, red, fawn, brindle, or any of these with white patches.
Photos: 3, 10, 14, 15 & 17

Ibizan Hound

From 60-66cm (23-26 inches) in height. Weight is around 22kg (48 pounds). The coat is smooth, tough and long haired. Usually orange and white, fawn, red, or red and white in color.
Photos: 6, 8, 9, 11 & 13

TERRIERS

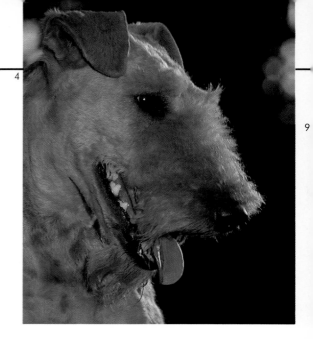

TIBETAN TERRIER
SOFT COATED WHEATEN
WELSH TERRIER

The **Tibetan Terrier,** or Chrysanthemum Dog, is an older breed than the Tibetan Spaniel, Lhasa Apso and Shi-Tzu, but related to them. It also looks very like a miniature Old English Sheepdog. A lively, gentle and affectionate dog, its size and temperament make it a particularly good pet, and with its deep bark and alert attitude it is also an effective little watchdog.

The **Soft Coated Wheaten** is a terrier from Ireland. An ideal country dog, it is a natural hunter, good at herding sheep and as a watchdog. Not the best known of terriers from Great Britain, it is a lively, courageous, obedient and adaptable dog. It gets its name from the color of its coat which is, most usually, the color of ripe wheat. Not seen much in international competition, it is, however, a faithful companion.

The **Welsh Terrier** is closely related to the Fox Terrier. A British dog, the breed is a cross of certain terriers with the Airedale, of which it is a small version. Over the years it has gone from being a country dog used for otter hunting to a pet and show dog. It has many strings to its bow: on dry land and underground it has all the skills of a terrier, but it is also at home in the water. In addition it is a dog which adapts easily to life in an apartment, to living with children and a quiet life generally.

Tibetan Terrier

From 30-32cm (12-13 inches) in height. Weight should not exceed 15kg (35 pounds). The coat is luxuriant, the long fur over the eyes hanging down like the petals of a large Chrysanthemum flower, hence the nickname. The coat may be any shade from white through the grays to black.

Photos: 1, 5, 7 & 9

Soft Coated Wheaten

From 30-40cm (11-15 inches) in height. Weight is 15-18kg (33-40 pounds). The coat is thick and soft and slightly curling or wavy. Wheat colored.

Photos: 2, 8, 10, 11, 13 & 16

Welsh Terrier

From 37-40cm (14-16 inches) in height. Weight is 8-9.5kg (18-20 pounds). The coat is full, thick and rough and may be black and tan or gray and tan.

Photos: 3, 4, 6, 12, 14 & 16

GERMAN HUNT TERRIER
WEST HIGHLAND WHITE TERRIER
SKYE TERRIER

The **German Hunt Terrier,** while a German breed, is the result of crossing a number of British terriers. A hunter by instinct, it has the reputation of being extremely savage with its prey and will attack any small animal, including cats. Naturally aggressive and therefore a good watchdog, it cannot be recommended as a family pet.

The **West Highland White Terrier** is from the same group as the Skye Terrier but is most closely related to the Cairn Terrier, being originally, in fact, a white Cairn. Fable has it that white Cairns used to be destroyed as not true Cairns, until in the 19th century a Scottish Laird discovered that the white dogs showed up much better when hunting in the rain and mists of the mountains, and he started to breed them under the name of West Highland White. The "Westie," as it is affectionately known, has a mischievous look and loves people, particularly children. It enjoys the open air and the country but makes an excellent home-loving pet.

The **Skye Terrier** is one of the oldest of the short legged terrier breeds. So called because it comes from the island of Skye in Scotland, many legends surround its origins: some say it is descended from a Maltese Terrier that was rescued from the wreck of a Spanish ship. A good hunter, watchdog and sheepdog, it was used in Britain for (now illegal) badger hunting. A brave little dog, like all terriers, the Skye makes a faithful companion but does not like to be shut in. Despite its size it is not a dog that should be kept in a small apartment.

13

14

German Hunt Terrier
They grow to around 40cm (15 inches) in height. Weight is 7-9kg (15-19 pounds). The coat may be smooth or rough and is usually gray or black in color.
Photos: 1, 3, 5 & 11

West Highland White Terrier
From 20-30cm (8-11 inches) in height. Weight is 8-10kg (17-22 pounds). The coat is rough, particularly on the underside, and always pure white.
Photos: 2, 6, 8, 10, 12, 13 & 16

16

17

Skye Terrier
Height is around 25cm (10 inches). Weight is 6-11kg (13-24 pounds). The coat is heavy, straight and long, hanging right down to the ground. May be gray, blue or fawn in color. The ears are always black.
Photos: 4, 7, 9, 14, 15 & 17

15

BOSTON TERRIER
CAIRN TERRIER
LAKELAND TERRIER

The **Boston Terrier** is, of course, an American dog and is a cross between a British Bulldog and a white English terrier. The Boston Terrier Club of America was formed in 1891 and the breed was accepted by the American Kennel Club in 1893. Despite being classified with the Terrier group, this dog, with its surprising physique, looks much more like a miniature mastiff, with its flat face, pointed ears and short, smooth coat. The blood of many breeds runs in its veins, giving it a distinctive personality. It has none of the usual hunting instincts of the terrier group but is a dog that loves to play with children and adults alike. Not at all aggressive, it is comfortable living in a small space and is at home in the city or the country. More of a toy dog than a terrier, it is a perfect pet.

The **Cairn Terrier,** a Scottish breed, is one of the small terriers. A good country dog and a good hunter, it has a lovely temperament, lively and affectionate. Unlike some terriers it is not aggressive and does not need a great deal of exercise. Very attached to its owners, and full of fun, the Cairn makes a rewarding and enchanting pet.

The **Lakeland Terrier** comes from the Lake District of England. This little terrier is from an ancient breed once used for otter hunting and is at home in difficult or marshy ground. Today it is a show dog, enjoying the competition ring. Popular in Britain, its handsome appearance has brought the Lakeland many prizes in important British shows.

Boston Terrier

From 25-43cm (10-17 inches) in height. Weight is 7-12.5kg (15-27 pounds). The coat is fine, short and shiny, black and white in color or brindle with white patches.

Photos: 1, 5, 7, 9, 13 & 15

Cairn Terrier

Maximum height is 30cm (11 inches). Weight is 5-7kg (11-15 pounds). Rough coated, the fur is soft and plentiful and may be red, sandy, silver and black or brindle in color.

Photos: 3, 8, 10, 11, 12, 14 & 16

Lakeland Terrier

Around 36cm (14 inches) in height and about 8kg (17 pounds) in weight. The coat is rough and thick and may be any color except white.

Photos: 2, 4, 6 & 17

FOX TERRIER • AIREDALE

There are two types of **Fox Terrier**: the Smooth Haired and the Wire Haired. The British Smooth Haired Fox Terrier is a true hunt terrier: a fearless fighter, proud of its ancient lineage. This breed has been known in Europe since Roman times. The American Fox Terrier Club was formed in 1885. An independent, quarrelsome, clever dog that makes its presence felt, it is also a sparky, fun little dog with a reliable temperament. The rough haired Fox terrier has the same fighting and hunting instincts. An elegant, well-muscled dandy of the dog world, with an impertinent little beard, it loves to show off. Notoriously obstinate, these little dogs like their own way, but once mastered make excellent watchdogs who love to bark.

The **Airedale**, like most of the terrier group, is another British dog. It gets its name from the river in the the county of Yorkshire. Standing tall on the tips of its toes, the slim but muscular Airedale is always active and can run very fast. Tireless and fearless, it will take on much stronger foes than itself and has not forgotten that its ancestors hunted bear and wolves. Today it is used in certain parts of Europe to hunt wild boar and deer. This talented dog has proved efficient at many jobs: wartime messenger, police dog, seeing-eye dog, watchdog and hunter. Today it makes a great pet which loves to play detective around its home.

Fox Terrier

Around 40cm (16 inches) in height and 8-9kg (17-19 pounds) in weight. The coat may be smooth and thick or rough and curly. Predominantly white in color with brown and gray patches.

Photos (rough haired): **1, 3, 8, 10, 14 & 17**

(smooth haired): **5, 11, 13 & 16**

Airedale

From 55-61cm (22-24 inches) in height and around 20kg (44 pounds) in weight. The coat is rough and thick. The body color is black or gray with reddish brown head, tail and paws.

Photos: 2, 4, 6, 7, 9, 12 & 15

DANDY DINMONT TERRIER
IRISH TERRIER
MANCHESTER TERRIER

The **Dandy Dinmont Terrier** is an ancient breed whose name came from a terrier character in Sir Walter Scott's novel *Guy Mannering*. The first Dandy Dinmont Club was formed in 1876. Even if its physique is not strictly that of a typical terrier, it certainly has the temperament of a true catcher of rats and other small animals, such as moles, mice and weasels. Happy in all kinds of surroundings, it is fun, affectionate and sociable with those close to it, but reserved with strangers. The Dandy Dinmont has laughing eyes and a distinctive tuft of hair on the top of its head, which gives it an amusing appearance.

The **Irish Terrier** first saw the light of day in the early 19th century in Ireland and was bred from dogs which must have been closely related to the rough haired Fox Terrier. Its nickname is "Red Devil" because of its color and bravery. A slender, elegant dog, this wild Irish creature can be very fierce when tracking or hunting small prey or when used (as it once was) as a fighting dog. It appears to be a many talented dog: a great hunter and gun dog with a gentle, affectionate, easily-managed temperament as well. Much sought after in Great Britain and Ireland.

The **Manchester Terrier** is an English dog, the result of crossing the Black and Tan Terrier and the Italian Greyhound. The breed is beginning to disappear despite the desperate efforts of its supporters to prevent this. A champion rat catcher, it is also an excellent pet: sweet tempered, intelligent and affectionate, but curiously not very popular.

11

8

12

15

9

13

16

14

Dandy Dinmont Terrier
From 20-25cm (8-10 inches) in height. The coat is rough haired and sticks up. Usually sandy and black in color.
Photos: 1, 5, 6, 7, 8, 10, 11, 14, 15 & 16

Irish Terrier
From 35-46cm (14-18 inches) in height and 9-12kg (20-26 pounds) in weight. The coat is rough, thick and wavy and usually red in color.
Photos: 3, 9 & 12

Manchester Terrier
Around 25cm (10 inches) in height and 8kg (17 pounds) in weight. The coat is short, thick, straight and shiny. Black in color with red on the head and chest.
Photos: 2, 4 & 13

10

BEDLINGTON TERRIER
SCOTTISH TERRIER · BULL TERRIER
JACK RUSSELL TERRIER

The **Bedlington Terrier** is the only dog that really looks like a lamb! But this pure-bred English terrier has all the characteristics of the true terrier. Despite its fragile and rather amusing appearance, it was once a formidable hunter of small prey, from rats and mice to badgers. It was also used in the mines to clear the tunnels of rats and was a prized poacher's dog. Looking something like a curly whippet, this is a dog with all the skills of the hunter, watchdog and everyday companion. Nowadays it is perfectly happy being curled and combed and prepared for the show ring, and it loves all the attention.

The **Scottish Terrier** is Scottish by name and typically Scottish in temperament. Dark colored, with a square-shaped head, it has pointed ears and a little beard under its chin. A great hunter, despite its short legs, the "Scotty" is a robust, weatherproof, indefatigable and obstinate dog. Afraid of nothing, it makes a great watchdog but, strangely, rarely barks. Properly trained it makes a wonderful family pet that gets on well with children.

The **Bull Terrier** is an English dog, probably a cross between the English Bulldog and a terrier of some kind. It has an amusing, oblong-shaped head and a strong, stocky body. Its physique made it a natural fighting dog in times past. Once cruel and bloodthirsty, it is now tamed and civilized enough to make a good pet, while still being an excellent watchdog.

The **Jack Russell Terrier** is an English dog which gets its name from the 19th century vicar, the Reverend Jack Russell, who bred them from certain Fox Terriers whose lines he particularly admired. Now shorter legged than the original Jack Russells, the breed has ears that turn down and a sweet expression. Although small the Jack Russell is great at flushing out small game. Still unrecognized in the official American terrier classifications, the breed has recently been accepted by the British Kennel Club.

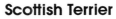

Bedlington Terrier

Around 40cm (15 inches) in height and 8-10kg (17-22 pounds) in weight. The coat is rough, thick and lightly curling. May be blue, sable, gray, blue, gray or chocolate in color.
Photos: 2, 4, 8, 12, 15 & 17

Scottish Terrier

From 25-30cm (10-12 inches) in height and 7-10kg (15-22 pounds) in weight. The coat is thick, with a beard, luxuriant eyebrows and mustache. Usually black in color but may also be creamy white.
Photos: 1, 3, 7 & 13

Bull Terrier

From 35-45cm (14-18 inches) in height and 18-20kg (39-44 pounds) in weight. The coat is very short, coarse and shiny. Usually white, sometimes with a patch over the eye, or brindle.
Photos: 5, 6, 10 & 14

Jack Russell Terrier

Around 22cm (9 inches) in height and 4-5kg (8-11 pounds) in weight. The coat is coarse and straight and may be rough or smooth haired. White in color with black or tan patches.
Photos: 9, 11 & 16

SLED DOGS

ALASKAN MALEMUTE ESKIMO DOG

The **Alaskan Malemute,** the best known of the sled dog group, had its standard issued by the American Kennel Club in 1927. With its slit eyes and large head, to children it can look like a wolf. The strongest and most hardy of the sled dogs, it is in perfect harmony with its environment of snow, wide open spaces and severe cold. Not as fast as the Siberian Husky, but with more endurance, it is used for sled racing over short distances. It also hunts caribou, seals and bears. It gets its name from the Eskimo Malemute tribe. Its origins and way of life, constantly surrounded by people, have made it deeply attached to humans and therefore an excellent companion. A powerful, courageous dog with a well developed sense of direction and subtle instincts. Immortalized as the sled dogs in Jack London's *Call of the Wild*, Alaskan Malemutes are the symbol of adventure in the frozen North.

The **Eskimo Dog** belongs to the Spitz group from Polar regions. A descendant (like its cousins the Siberian Husky, Samoyede and Alaskan Malemute) of the boreal wolf, it is found mostly in Greenland and the Mackenzie Basin. Since time immemorial it has run in harness. Full of energy, a fighter, hardy and very fast, it has all the qualities necessary for crossing vast distances at speed while pulling a heavy load. It does not like the heat or a sedentary life and, while not an aggressive dog, was certainly not meant to be kept indoors. It needs the open spaces.

Alaskan Malemute

From 55-67cm (21-26 inches) in height and 30-38kg (66-84 pounds) in weight. The coat is very thick and soft and may be wolf gray or black and white.
Photos: 1, 3, 7, 12, 13, 14 & 15

Eskimo Dog

May be over 60cm (24 inches) in height for a male dog and not less than 55cm (21 inches) for a female. The coat is straight and rough and may be any color except all white.
Photos: 2, 4, 5, 6, 8, 9, 10, 11 & 16

SIBERIAN HUSKY

The **Siberian Husky** belongs to the same group of Polar dogs as the Samoyede, Alaskan Malemute and the Eskimo Dog. It is by far the most sought after of the four because of its startling, azure-blue eyes, its energy and rhythmic stride when working in a harness team. It long ago overtook the Malemute in this respect. The first team of Siberian huskies appeared in the All Alaska Sweepstakes race of 1909. A native of Siberia, it was imported into Alaska at the turn of the century. Affectionate, gentle and extremely attached to its owner, it can, however, show a determination to get its own way. Its need for open spaces, a good run and enough

exercise to tire it out must be respected if it is to be kept as a pet. A magnificent and very beautiful dog, it is not a toy and should not be treated as such. Much sought after in the showing world for its incredible blue eyes outlined in black.

0

13

14

15

1

16

Siberian Husky

From 51-60cm (20-24 inches) in height and 22-27kg (48-60 pounds) in weight. The coat is thick and smooth and insulates the dog from the arctic temperatures of its normal habitat. From dark gray, through silver to black in color.

Photos: 1 to 17

2

17

SAMOYEDE • JAPANESE SPITZ SWEDISH SPITZ

The **Samoyede** comes from Siberia and gets its name from the Samoyede people who used it to pull sleds. This dog, with its pure white coat, is used to the great open spaces of the frozen North and to carrying out really hard tasks. Solidly built, it is neither aggressive nor vicious, despite the breed's relatively hard and wild way of life. With a calm, gentle, obedient nature it is, despite its origins, perfectly happy living a city life, even in an apartment. But since it is, like all Spitzes, a descendant of the boreal wolf, it is probably best not to shut it up too much.

The **Japanese Spitz,** or Hokkaido Spitz, was a dog of the Ainu people of Japan. Descended from sled dogs, it takes its name from the Island of Hokkaido, home of the Ainu. The breed has kept the sturdiness, speed and qualities of endurance of a sled dog. Once a hunter of bear and a watchdog, it is today, first and foremost, an excellent pet; a faithful and affectionate companion that loves family life.

The **Swedish Spitz,** or Norbotten Spitz, belongs to the sled dog group but its origins are unknown. Rather small, it has a strong, muscular body and an ever-watchful look about it. Essentially a sled dog and a watchdog, although affectionate and faithful it is very efficient against thieves, being always on the lookout for trouble.

7

11

8

Samoyede

From 48-60cm (19-23 inches) in height and 23-30kg (50-66 pounds) in weight. The coat looks soft and pliable but is actually rough to the touch. Usually pure white in color.
Photos: 1, 2, 4, 6, 8, 9, 10, 11 & 13

Japanese Spitz

From 41-50cm (16-19 inches) in height. Around 25kg (55 pounds) in weight. The coat is straight and soft and red, black, white or any of these flecked, in color.
Photos: 3, 7 & 12

Swedish Spitz

There is no standard size and weight. Characterized by very pointed ears and a long, curly tail. The coat is rough and white in color with yellow or reddish brown patches.
Photo: 5

9

12

13

10

GUN DOGS

WEIMARANER • COCKER SPANIEL
ITALIAN SPINONE
RHODESIAN RIDGEBACK

The **Weimaraner** is a German dog that should not be confused with the German Pointer. Its origin is much disputed but it is probably the result of crossing certain German and French hunting breeds. It is, however, an ancient breed noted for its elegant and powerful appearance. In 1929 an American sportsman, Howard White, brought a pair to the United States and the American Weimaraner Club was formed. Nowadays mostly docked, the tiny stump of a tail on this large dog looks a little strange. First and foremost a natural hunter, it is an excellent gun dog and retriever. In the United States it is nicknamed the "Gray Ghost" because of its speed and light color.

The English **Cocker Spaniel** is the most popular of all the English Spaniels and is famous the world over. Like all Spaniels, its ancestors must have been Spanish dogs. The American Kennel Club recognized it as a separate breed in 1943. With its big, pendulous, curly-haired ears, loving expression and ability to charm everyone, it is adored by its owners, who usually pamper and spoil it. But, contrary to modern beliefs, it is in fact an excellent gun dog, a good retriever of game and a working dog rather than a pet. In Europe it is used mostly in game bird shooting. Very sought after as a pet, it does need a lot of exercise and is not very good on its own with small children. An artful charmer, with a roguish and loving look, it knows how to get around its owner and can get away with anything by batting its eyelids!

The **Italian Spinone** dates back to the 15th century. A country dog, with well developed muscles and very hardy, it combines the qualities of an excellent hunter with those of a faithful pet.

The **Rhodesian Ridgeback,** also called the African Lion Hound, comes from Southern Africa. Bred by the Boers, this dog has a unique feature: an arrow-shaped line of hair running the length of the spinal column. Used to hunt big game.

Weimaraner

From 57-60cm (22-24 inches) in height and 25-28kg (55-62 pounds) in weight. The smooth, soft coat may be all shades of bluey gray or browny gray and it may be long or short haired.

Photos: 1, 3, 5 & 12

Cocker Spaniel

From 37-41cm (14-16 inches) in height and 11-13kg (24-28 pounds) in weight. The coat is flat, smooth and silky and slightly wavy. All colors are permitted.

Photos: 2, 4, 6, 7, 9, 13, 14 & 15

Italian Spinone

From 58-70cm (23-27 inches) in height and 28-37kg (60-80 pounds) in weight. The coat is rough and spiky, hence its name, from the Italian *Spino*, meaning spine or thorn. The coat is cream, with orange, white or chocolate flecks or patches.

Photos: 8 & 10

Rhodesian Ridgeback

From 61-68.5cm (24-27 inches) in height and 29.5-34kg (65-75 pounds) in weight. The coat is short, thick and shiny, sandy or tan in color.

Photos: 11 & 16

BRITTANY SPANIEL
ENGLISH POINTER
FRENCH POINTER
PICARDY SPANIEL

The **Brittany Spaniel** is the best known French gun dog. Recognized by the American Kennel Club in 1931, it is one of the most popular working gundogs in the United States. Intelligent, roguish and affectionate, it is also a sensitive, solidly-built and hardy dog. It is best at retrieving game birds.

The **English Pointer** is one of the handsomest of the gun dog group and is the archetype of all pointers. The present day breed is a mixture of the original English pointer with a little French and Spanish blood thrown in, resulting in a dog of many qualities: beauty, nobility, intelligence and extraordinary hunting skills. It is the aristocrat of gun dogs, good at catching and retrieving game. A great athlete too, the English Pointer is both courageous and gentle with children. As long as its need for space and exercise is respected, it makes a great pet.

The **French Spaniel,** while coming from France, is not in fact as typically French a dog as the Brittany Spaniel and is known beyond the frontiers of Europe. A good gun dog, it hunts all furred and feathered game and makes an excellent pet, being gentle, affectionate and patient by nature.

The **Picardy Spaniel** was a gun dog in danger of becoming extinct, and it has only recently been saved. A retriever of water fowl, it is a gentle, sensitive and easy-to-look-after dog.

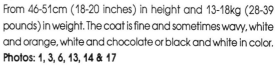

Brittany Spaniel

From 46-51cm (18-20 inches) in height and 13-18kg (28-39 pounds) in weight. The coat is fine and sometimes wavy, white and orange, white and chocolate or black and white in color.
Photos: 1, 3, 6, 13, 14 & 17

English Pointer

From 54-67cm (21-26 inches) in height and 20-30kg (44-66 pounds) in weight. The coat is very short, smooth and fine. May be black and white, white and yellow or white and reddish brown in color. Single colors are also found.
Photos: 4, 5, 8, 9 & 15

French Spaniel

From 54-60cm (21-23 inches) in height and 20-25kg (44-55 pounds) in weight. The coat is long, flat or slightly wavy. White in color with reddish brown patches.
Photos: 10 & 11

Picardy Spaniel

From 55-60cm (21-23 inches) in height and around 20kg (44 pounds) in weight. The coat is thick and slightly wavy. White with reddish brown flecks in color.
Photos: 2, 7, 12 & 16

IRISH SETTER
LABRADOR RETRIEVER
GORDON SETTER

The **Irish Setter** is known to everyone and much admired for its flamboyant red color and thoroughbred looks. Its ancient origins include some Pointer and some Spanish Spaniel blood. A remarkable hunter; fast, hardy and with an exceptional ability to follow a scent, it will hunt pheasant, partridge and duck as happily as it will hunt rabbit. It is a dog with a lot of character and is not easy to train, being rather determined to get its own way, unless it has a strong owner. But just the same, the Irish Setter makes a wonderful pet as long as it is not kept in the city. It needs a lot of exercise and if kept shut up it soon becomes unmanageable.

The **Labrador Retriever** is a British dog, imported from Newfoundland in the 19th century. It has undergone a remarkable change, being taught by the English to retrieve game as successfully on land as it once caught fish in the cold waters of its homeland. It is extremely popular in the United States. Stocky and endearingly clumsy, with a waddling gait, the labrador is a dog which looks strong, hardy and pugnacious. It has many skills: as a gun dog (being as good over water as on dry land), as an excellent sniffer dog for drugs, as a seeing-eye dog for the blind and a wonderful, faithful pet which loves family life.

The **Gordon Setter** is an English dog bred from Scottish lines, with a number of different Setters and Collies in its ancestry. Not as elegant as the Irish Setter, it is a country dog which can cover remarkable distances, and it makes a good watchdog.

9

13

10

Irish Setter

From 54-72cm (21-28 inches) in height and 18-27kg (39-59 pounds) in weight. Medium to long haired, the coat is short over the ears and paws. Usually reddish brown, one colored.
Photos: 1, 2, 10, 11 & 13

Labrador Retriever

From 54-57cm (20-21 inches) in height and 25-30kg (55-66 pounds) in weight. The coat is short, thick, straight and coarse. May be cream, black, chocolate or yellow in color, but always single colored.
Photos: 3, 4, 6, 7, 12 & 16

11

14

Gordon Setter

From 56-66cm (22-26 inches) in height and 24-30kg (52-66 pounds) in weight. The coat is smooth, silky and slightly wavy. Black and red in color.
Photos: 5, 8, 9, 14 & 15

12

15

16

WATER SPANIEL
NOVA SCOTIA RETRIEVER
CLUMBER SPANIEL
CURLY COATED RETRIEVER

The **Water Spaniel** is a French dog. Not very well known to the public, this retriever is often confused with a sheepdog, thanks to its resemblance to such breeds as the Bearded Collie and the Old English Sheepdog. The breed is in danger of becoming extinct but it is a dog of many qualities: a great hunter in water and an excellent pet, even though it is a large dog which likes the open air and needs a lot of exercise.

The **Nova Scotia Retriever** is a Canadian dog which is practically unknown in Europe. A wonderful swimmer, it is also intelligent and powerful.

The **Clumber Spaniel** is an English gun dog which has become sought after in Britain since one of the breed won the championship at Crufts (the top British dog show) a few years ago. One of the aristocrats of the Spaniel world, it has a distinctive physique: short legged, with a large head on a short neck, a flattened muzzle and massive build. Unaggressive in temperament, almost debonair, it is a calm, quiet dog. As well as being an excellent gun dog, it makes a lovely (though still not well known) companion.

The **Curly Coated Retriever** is one of the handsomest of the British retriever breeds. It arrived in the United States in about 1907. A careful cross between a Newfoundland, a Labrador and a Poodle, it is a tall, slim, elegant dog with a distinctive, tightly-curling coat, and is full of character. Not as popular as the Flat Coated Retriever, however. As much at home in the water as on dry land, the Curly Coated Retriever is particularly good when accompanying duck hunters.

Water Spaniel

Around 60cm (24 inches) in height and 20-25kg (44-55 pounds) in weight. The coat is medium long, coarse haired and untidy. Gray, black or chocolate in color with white markings.

Photos: 2, 3, 5, 8, 9 & 16

Nova Scotia Retriever

From 43-55cm (17-21 inches) in height. Around 25kg (55 pounds) in weight. The coat is medium long and straight haired. Sandy colored with a white shirt front.

Photos: 4, 6, 12 & 15

Clumber Spaniel

From 28-32cm (11-13 inches) in height and 20-31kg (44-68 pounds) in weight. The coat is silky and hangs straight. Creamy white in color with orangy patches.

Photos: 10. 11 & 17

Curly Coated Retriever

Maximum is 65cm (26 inches) in height and weight should be 31-36kg (68-79 pounds). The thick coat is tightly curled all over and is black or chocolate in color.

Photos: 1, 7, 13 & 14

ENGLISH SETTER
FRENCH POINTER
AUVERGNE POINTER
SAINT GERMAIN POINTER

The **English Setter,** an unquestionably British breed, has all the qualities of the Setter group: beauty, speed, elegance and brilliance at flushing out game. It is particularly good at hunting woodcock, perhaps the most difficult game bird of all. Both by eyesight and instinct it is particularly suited to the job. It is even able to retrieve fallen Woodcock, which are notoriously difficult to find, being so well camouflaged. It is a gun dog first and foremost and, if kept as a pet, in which role it will be quite happy, its need for open spaces and a well regulated life must be respected.

The **French Pointer** is a breed whose origins go back to the 17th century. There are two types: the Gascony Pointer and the Pyrenean. The French are famous for their gundogs and there are many different Pointer, Spaniel and Retriever breeds from France. This one is both an excellent gundog and pet, being sturdy and elegant.

The **Auvergne Pointer** may not be a pure French breed, possibly having some Maltese blood in its ancestry. It is considered to be the fastest of the French hunting dogs, always keen to quarter the ground for game or marsh birds. Unworried by cold or stormy weather, it is also a home-loving family dog.

The **Saint Germain Pointer** dates back to the 19th century. This elegant and aristocratic dog hunts rabbit and pheasant and is at home in woodland. Not as popular as it might be, given its excellent skills as a gundog.

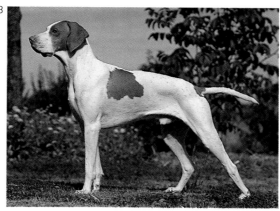

English Setter
From 55-63cm (24-27 inches) in height and 22-25kg (55-66 pounds) in weight. The coat is silky, wavy and fine haired, with long fringes on the body and legs. White in color with black or blue/gray flecks and patches and sometimes a third color.
Photos: 2, 3, 6, 8, 9, 12 & 14

French Pointer
Gascony Pointer: from 57-69cm (22-27 inches) in height and 25-32kg (55-70 pounds) in weight. Pyrenean Pointer: from 49-60cm (19-23 inches) in height and 17-25kg (37-55 pounds) in weight. The Gascony breed has a rough, thick coat, usually white in color with chocolate patches. The Pyrenean breed has a short, fine haired coat, usually chocolate with white markings on the head, shirt front and tips of the paws.
Photos: 4, 7, 11 & 15

Auvergne Pointer
From 55-63cm (24-25 inches) in height and 22-25kg (48-55 pounds) in weight. The coat is short and shiny. White in color with small, black or chocolate spots and patches.
Photos: 1, 5, 10 & 16

Saint Germain Pointer
From 50-62cm (19-24 inches) in height and 18-26kg (39-57 pounds) in weight. The coat is long and straight, a dull white in color flecked with orange.
Photo: 13

FLAT COATED RETRIEVER
GERMAN POINTER
CHIEN D'ARTOIS
GRIFFON KORTHALS

The **Flat Coated Retriever** is an English gundog. Good at retrieving in water; a legacy from the Newfoundland in its ancestry. It also has some Labrador, Irish Setter and other blood in its veins. A typically British dog: loving and patient and therefore a great pet as well as being a skilled gun dog over all kinds of terrain.

The **German Pointer** was first registered in the United States in 1930 and there are two distinct types: the German Shorthaired Pointer and the German Wirehaired Pointer. Extremely popular in its own country, it is probably descended from the Spanish Pointer and the English Pointer. One of the best gundogs around, it is fast, able to cope with any kind of terrain, and has an amazing instinct for game. Both handsome and effective, it possesses all the qualities that please, including getting on with children, which makes it an excellent family pet, but it does need plenty of walks in the fresh air.

The **Chien d'Artois** is a French dog with some British blood (Fox Hound and Basset Hound) in its veins. It is characterized by long, pendulous ears and a sweet, slightly sad expression. Used for hunting hare, it can run fast and over long distances in any type of country.

The **Griffon Korthals,** bred by a Dutchman, is a remarkable retriever. This gundog is the result of crosses between Spaniel, Griffon, English Setter, Otterhound and German Pointer. It has inherited the best qualities of all of these and is used as an all purpose gundog. A champion at hunting hare and quail.

8

17

9

13

Flat Coated Retriever

May grow to 66cm (26 inches) in height and 32kg (70 pounds) in weight. The coat is flat, fine haired and very shiny. Black or reddish brown in color.
Photos: 1, 6, 8, 9 &13

German Pointer

May grow to 66cm (26 inches) in height and 30kg (66 pounds) in weight. The coat is short, rough and flat to the body. May be dark brown in color flecked with white, or vice-versa, or black with brown and white flecks.
Photos: 3, 5, 7, 15 & 17

0

14

Chien d'Artois

From 52-58cm (21-23 inches) in height and 25-30kg (55-66 pounds) in weight. The coat is short and coarse and tri-colored: white, reddish brown and dark tan.
Photos: 10, 12 & 16

Griffon Korthals

From 50-60cm (19-23 inches) in height and 23-27kg (50-60 pounds) in weight. The coat is rough and untidy, reddish brown, white or brownish gray in color.
Photos: 2, 4, 11 & 14

11

15

12

16

WATCHDOGS

DOBERMANN • BULLMASTIFF YUGOSLAVIAN CHARPLA

The **Dobermann,** a German breed, makes one of the best watchdogs both for the home or as a professional guard dog. One glimpse of its teeth is enough to stop anyone taking it on! It was first used as a trained guard dog towards the end of the 19th century by a customs officer, Louis Dobermann, who found it a good persuader when collecting revenues. The Doberman is a cross of many breeds: Pinscher, Mastiff, Rottweiler and Manchester Terrier, from the letter of which it gets its coloring. The popular view of the Dobermann is of an aggressive guard dog, vicious and liking to bite. This impression is not helped by it being frequently pictured in movies going for the throat of the bad guy. The reality is very different; properly trained and with a firm owner, the "Dobey" is a loving, manageable animal. In the United States it is a very popular police dog.

The **Bullmastiff** is an English dog, a smaller version of the Mastiff. It was recognized by the American Kennel Club in 1933. An impressive dog with its huge head, dark muzzle and piercing gaze, it is at the same time affectionate and cuddly, with a lazy side to its character. Centuries ago it resulted from a cross with the Bulldog, which is still clearly visible in its make up. An excellent watchdog (even used by the police in parts of Europe), it makes a great pet, provided it is well trained and the owner is in control. It is a fun, intelligent dog that loves its home and family. Strangers should beware of upsetting the Bullmastiff however; they would soon be sorry!

The **Yugoslavian Charpla,** or Illyrian Sheepdog, originated in the East. Also known as the Charplaninatz, it makes a ferocious watchdog by night and a cuddly pet by day, but one always ready to leap at the throat of any wolf which threatens its flock. A popular watchdog and sheepdog in its own country.

13

14

17

15

18

Dobermann

From 61-70cm (24-27 inches) in height and around 25kg (55 pounds) in weight. The coat is close cropped, coarse and shiny. May be black, blue or chocolate in color with red markings.

Photos: 1, 4, 6, 7, 9, 14, 16 & 17

Bullmastiff

May grow to 70cm (27 inches) in height and around 65kg (140 pounds) in weight. The coat is close cropped and thick and usually light in color: fawn or golden.

Photos: 2, 10, 12, 13 & 18

Yugoslavian Charpla

From 50-60cm (19-23 inches) in height and 25-45kg (55-95 pounds) in weight. The coat is long, thick and soft: iron gray in color.

Photos: 3, 5, 8, 11 & 15

16

ROTTWEILER • BOXER MALINOIS

The **Rottweiler** is a German dog, bred to look after cattle and sheep. There is mastiff, hound, and some ancient sheepdog blood in its veins, and it is said to be a descendant of the huge hounds of ancient Greece and Rome. However, it long since quit the south for the northern climes of Europe and is now a native of Switzerland and Southern Wurtemburg. It has a solid, very powerful build, with a terrifying set of teeth and a formidable temperament. It is wise not to approach a Rottweiler that you don't know. Its remarkable physical qualities are reinforced by considerable intelligence, courage and willingness. A good guardian of its flocks, it excels as a watchdog and professional guard dog. But it also loves family life and children and will defend these to the death if necessary.

The **Boxer** is another German dog. Its early ancestors, also German, hunted wild boar and bear and guarded flocks. Those who know the Boxer will confirm that it is an exuberant, fun-loving, playful, high-spirited animal that will happily knock you over in its attempts to show you how much it loves you! It is intelligent, faithful and very capable of looking after its home, despite its equable temperament.

The **Malinois** is a Belgian sheepdog, which much resembles the German Shepherd at first sight. The breed was almost lost during the second World War and has only survived thanks to crossing a few surviving Malinois with Groenendaels, which it also resembles. Rather self willed, it is necessary to understand how to handle the Malinois, but they make excellent watchdogs and pets.

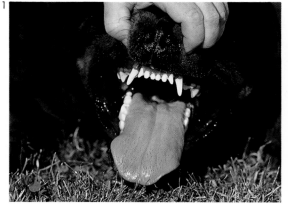

13

14

18

15

16

Rottweiler

From 60-65cm (24-26 inches) in height and around 30kg (60 pounds) standard weight (though many considerably exceed this). The coat is short and rough to the touch. Usually black in color with red markings or black with sandy markings or vice versa.

Photos: 1, 3, 9, 11, 14 & 16

Boxer

From 57-60cm (22-24 inches) in height and 24-32kg (52-70 pounds) in weight. The coat is close cropped and shiny. Fawn or brindle in color, with or without white markings.

Photos: 2, 10, 12, 13 & 18

Malinois

From 54-60cm (21-24 inches) in height The coat is short, dense and rough to the touch. Lightish brown in color.

Photos: 4, 5, 6, 7, 8, 15 & 17

17

FILA BRASILEIRO • LAPPHUND
AUSTRALIAN SHEEPDOG
NEAPOLITAN MASTIFF
ICELANDIC SPITZ

The **Fila Brasileiro,** as the name suggests, comes from South America. Probably the result of crosses between hounds imported by the conquerors of the New World and Bulldogs or Mastiffs. The Conquistadors used them to pursue escaped Indian slaves. An excellent sheepdog, the Fila Brasileiro is also a fierce watchdog. With its impressive appearance and characteristic gait, it is an elegant and supple dog. It prefers the great outdoors and life in the country to the city.

The **Lapphund,** or Lappland Sheepdog, is used as a watchdog and sheepdog in Lappland, but is in fact Swiss. It is probably the ancestor of the Spitz. Some say that these dogs, which look after reindeer herds in northern Finland, are still rather wild. The Lapplanders use them for all kinds of jobs: as watchdogs, sheepdogs and pets. The Lapphund is a vigilant and agreeable companion, particularly good with children.

The **Australian Sheepdog** is the result of a cross between the Collie and the Dingo (the Australian wild dog). A very energetic, stocky and powerful dog.it is also docile and clever. Used to the wide open spaces of its home country, where it is used look after huge flocks of sheep and vast farms, it is *the* country dog.

The **Neapolitan Mastiff** is Italian, of course, and a descendant of the great hounds of Persia. Known throughout the Mediterranean area since ancient times, it even took part in events in the Roman arena. Despite the heavy jowls, which make it look like an old man, and its general air of calm, the Neapolitan Mastiff is a redoubtable watchdog which can be extremely ferocious. If you own one you need to master it, otherwise, watch out!

The **Icelandic Spitz** is a good sheepdog, excellent pet and also a great watchdog. Almost wiped out by disease, the breed was saved by breeders. Like all Spitzes, it is intelligent, loving and very attached to its owner.

Fila Brasileiro

Around 65cm (26 inches) in height and 50kg (110 pounds) in weight. The coat is short, smooth and soft. May be all colors.
Photos: 2, 6, 7, 9 & 11

Lapphund

Around 65cm (26 inches) in height and 20kg (44 pounds) in weight. The coat is long, straight and coarse. Usually black in color but may also be reddish brown with white markings.
Photos: 4 & 13

Australian Sheepdog

Around 48cm (19 inches) in height and 18-22kg (39-44 pounds) in weight. The coat is short and rough. The color ranges from blue, blue flecked, through to red flecked.
Photos: 8 & 13

Neapolitan Mastiff

From 65-75cm (26-29 inches) in height and around 70kg (150 pounds) in weight. The coat is close cropped and black, gray or brindle in color.
Photos: 3, 12 & 15

Icelandic Spitz

From 30-40cm (12-16 inches) in height and 9-13kg (20-28 pounds) in weight. The tail curls over the back. The coat is medium long and abundant. Tan, off white or black in color, with or without white markings.
Photos: 1, 5, 10 & 16

GERMAN SHEPHERD
BEAUCERON • HOVAWART

The **German Shepherd** is so well known that it really needs no introduction. A dog of excellent qualities and numerous skills, it is equally successful as a police dog, a seeing-eye dog for the blind, a loving guardian of its home and family and a faithful companion. Probably the most intelligent of dogs, it has a wonderful capacity for learning. Extremely adaptable, the same dog can be the fiercest of attack dogs under professional training and command one minute and a gentle, wholly reliable pet the next. Faithful and obedient, it is never happier than when trying to please, or take care of, its owner.

The **Beauceron,** a French dog bred as a sheepdog, makes a great watchdog. Its slightly aggressive nature makes it suspicious of strangers, and if left too long in an enclosed space it can become vicious. Generally, though, it is an intelligent dog whose aggression is easily controlled. Also known as the *Bas Rouge* (red socks) on account of the sock-like markings on its legs.

The **Hovawart** is a German dog, a working dog which in earlier times was used as a farm watchdog. Robust and heavy in build, it also makes a good rescue dog and seeing-eye dog for the blind. Deep chested and with an impressive set of teeth, despite its compact appearance it is also agile; running and jumping over obstacles with ease. Naturally intuitive, it also has a loud, penetrating bark, guaranteed to dissuade most intruders.

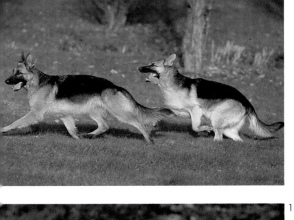

German Shepherd

Height varies from 55-60cm (22-27 inches) and it weighs from 30-50kg (66-110 pounds). The thick, straight coat can be long or short haired. It may be sable, tan and sable, silver or tan and gold in color.

Photos: 1, 5, 7, 11, 13 & 17

Beauceron

Around 70cm (27 inches) in height. Weight varies from 30-35kg (66-80 pounds). It has a heavy, short coat which can be black and red or, more commonly, black, red and silver.

Photos: 2, 3, 4, 6, 9 & 14

Hovawart

Can be as much as 70cm (27 inches) in height and weighs around 40kg (88 pounds). It has a longish, wavy coat which may be black, tan or golden.

Photos 8, 10, 12, 15 & 16

GREAT DANE • TIBETAN MASTIFF
DOGUE DE BORDEAUX

The **Great Dane,** also known as the German Mastiff, is nicknamed the "Apollo of the Canine world." Its origins are contested, but everyone agrees that it is an exceptionally handsome breed. The Great Dane Club of America was formed in Chicago in 1889. Tall, slim, well muscled, the Great Dane has a good temperament; ready to fly at the throat of an intruder it is otherwise a well-balanced, affectionate animal in normal circumstances. One of the best watchdogs.

The **Tibetan Mastiff** is an English dog, related to the true Tibetan Mastiff, still found in the Himalayas (where it is used as a watchdog). The British version has some crosses in its ancestry and is not a pure Tibetan Mastiff. It is a huge, massive dog with an impressive set of teeth and a large head. The Tibetan dog has the reputation of being very vicious, but this Western breed is more manageable, less aggressive, and happy with a disciplined way of life.

The **Dogue de Bordeaux,** or Bordeaux Mastiff, rather resembles a large Boxer. It has the same flattened muzzle and wrinkled face, the same shaped head and powerful, muscular body and deceptively fierce look. It can be extremely gentle with children and loves to play, though it is better to avoid being knocked down by this gentle giant. It has been used successfully as a police dog in France.

9

14

0

15

17

1

Great Dane

May grow to 90cm (36 inches) in height and weigh as much as 100kg (220 pounds)! The coat is short, straight and shiny and may be black, harlequin (black and white), brindle, blue gray or fawn in color.

Photos: 3-9 (harlequin), **11** (brindle), **6, 7, 10, 13 & 16**

Tibetan Mastiff

May grow to 80cm (31 inches) in height and weigh more than 80kg (175 pounds). The coat is coarse, medium long haired and black, yellow or red in color.

Photos: 2, 4, 8 & 15

2

16

Dogue de Bordeaux

From 54-68cm (21-26 inches) in height and around 50kg (120 pounds) in weight. The coat is fine, close cropped and soft, fawn in color.

Photos: 1, 5, 12, 14 & 17

3

ANGLO-FRENCH FOXHOUND
FRENCH HOUND

The **Anglo French Foxhound** does not have dual nationality as its name would suggest – it is a French dog. There are three types: Standard, Medium and Small. The English part of the name is a legacy from the English Harrier Hound blood found in the veins of the Standard and Medium Anglo-French and from the Beagle blood in the veins of the Small Anglo-French. This breed has kept the best hunting qualities of both nationalities and is much liked as a result. It has the keenness, speed and endurance of the English dog allied to the fearlessness of the French. The Medium and Small Anglo-French Foxhound is excellent at hunting hare, foxes and other small game. The Standard Anglo French, as well as being a handsome dog, has a remarkable instinct for the hunt and a fine voice, which from the 14th century onward has made it the star of royal deer and stag hunts in Europe.

All three types have the same physical characteristics of robustness and coloring, being tri-colored black, white and orange. These dogs, handsome as they are, do not make good pets. They need too much exercise and are essentially pack dogs which hate to live alone; they are bred to hunt.

The **French Hound** is a comparatively recent breed and a worthy addition to the hunting hound group. Used for stag and deer hunting, there are three types: Tri-colored; Black and White and Black and Orange, the latter the least well known of the three. This is a dog that is as ferocious and excitable at the hunt as it is calm and gentle at home.

Anglo-French Foxhound

The Standard and the Small are from 46-70cm (27-18 inches) in height and around 35kg (75 pounds) in weight for the Standard and 20kg (44 pounds) for the Small. The coat is close cropped and shiny. There are three different tri-colors.
Photos: 1, 7 & 12 (white and orange).

French Hound

The Tri-color is from 62-72cm (24-28 inches) in height and 28-30kg (60-66 pounds) in weight. The coat is short and black, red and white in color. The Black and White should be the same weight and size as the Standard but with a bi-colored coat. The strictly White and Orange variety is very rare and follows the same standard weight and size as the first two.
Photos: 4, 6, 8, 9, 13 & 15 (Black and White) **2, 3, 5, 10, 11 & 14** (White and Orange).

BLOODHOUND • OTTERHOUND
HAMILTON STOVARE • BILLY

The **Bloodhound** is a Belgian dog (known in that country as the Saint Hubert), imported into England at the Norman Conquest, at which time it also acquired its name. Its origins can be traced back to the 7th century, making it probably the oldest breed to hunt in a pack. There are several stories as to why it is called a Bloodhound, but most relate that it is in recognition of its pure, aristocratic blood lines. The Bloodhound was for centuries one of the best hunting dogs, following a scent brilliantly. Its excellent sense of smell made it a great pack dog and it is often used today by police to hunt down criminals. It is among the most physically powerful of the scent hounds, though it is not the speediest. A very popular dog in Europe and the United States, it is docile and easy to look after.

The **Otterhound** is a British dog first shown in the United States in 1907 in Oklahoma. It was bred to hunt Otters in the rivers and streams of Britain. Little known outside Britain, it is an enchanting dog with its long, rough coat and irresistibly charming expression. Bred to hunt in packs, if it is to be kept as a pet it must be given plenty of exercise and training to keep it a manageable dog.

The **Hamilton Stovare** is a Swedish scent hound. Good over difficult terrain and in pursuit of larger game.

The **Billy,** or Limousin Hound, is a French dog whose name sounds like a character from the Wild West, but in fact it comes from a small village in Poitou, France. First and foremost a pack hound, it does not make a good family dog and the breed is in danger of extinction.

12

13

Bloodhound

Around 67cm (27 inches) in height for the male and 60cm (23 inches) for the female. From 36-50kg (80-110 pounds) in weight. The coat is short, coarse and dense on the body and silky on the head and ears. Black and red is the most prized color but it may also be brown and red.

Photos: 3, 5, 8, 11 & 15

Otterhound

From 60-65cm (24-26 inches) in height and 30-35kg (66-76 pounds) in weight. The coat is rough and shiny. Gray, red, black or sandy in color with black and red patches.

Photos: 4, 10, 13 & 16

Hamilton Stovare

From 50-60cm (20-23 inches) in height and around 25kg (55 pounds) in weight. The coat is short, thick and tri-colored: black, brown and red.

Photos: 6 & 9

Billy

From 58-70cm (23-27 inches) in height and around 35kg (76 pounds) in weight. The coat is short, coarse and predominantly white, cream or white with orange patches.

Photos: 1, 2, 7, 12 & 14

14

15

16

BASSET HOUND
NORMANDY BASSET
BASSET FAUVE DE BRETAGNE
BASSET BLEU DE GASCOGNE

The **Basset** Hound arrived in the United States in 1863. Its origin goes back to a very early cross between a Basset from Europe and a Bloodhound. An enchantingly amusing dog to look at, with a body three times as long as it is high, a big head with long, pendulous ears and very sorrowful eyes. Beginning life as a pack dog, it is more often used today as a gundog in Europe and as a pet in the United States. General Lafayette is said to have made a gift of a Basset to George Washington. It has extremely well developed hunting instincts but makes an excellent pet provided it has plenty of exercise and fresh air; it is not a sedentary dog. Not always very manageable as it has a distinct liking for its own way and is not very friendly to those it does not know.

The **Normandy Basset** is a French dog closely related to the Basset Hound. With a never-ending body on short legs, it has the slightly comical charm of all Bassets. A dog bred for hunting, its small size is an advantage when seeking out prey gone to ground in inaccessible places. It makes a good companion for those who hunt but should not be kept in a confined space.

The **Basset Fauve de Bretagne** is another French Basset cross, this time between the Basset Vendeen and the Griffon Fauve de Bretagne. An ancient breed of pack dog, it nevertheless adapts well to life as a pet, having a calm and gentle temperament and is even happy in small living quarters.

The **Basset Bleu de Gascogne** is a cross of a number of Bassets and its origins are now uncertain. It is the smallest of the Gascony Bassets and is used for hunting game birds. An active, intelligent and easily-managed little dog.

1

2

3

4

6

7

8

9

Basset Hound

From 28-36cm (11-14 inches) in height. There is no standard weight. Weight varies enormously as the Basset is inclined to get fat easily. The skin is loose and very wrinkled. The coat is coarse haired but flat and thick. Bi-colored or tri-colored, they may be any of the normal hunting dog colors.

Photos: 5, 6, 7, 11 & 13

Normandy Basset

From 26-36cm (10-14 inches) in height. There is no standard weight. The coat is rough and close cropped and may be tri-colored: fawn, with white and orange patches, or bi-colored white and orange.

Photos: 1, 3, 12, 15 & 17

Basset Fauve de Bretagne

From 32-36cm (12-14 inches) in height and 16-18kg (35-40 pounds) in weight. The coat is short, thick and flat. Wheaten or fawn in color.

Photos: 2, 4, 8 & 14

Basset Bleu de Gascogne

From 34-42cm (13-16 inches) in height and 16-18kg (35-40 pounds) in weight. The coat is thick and blue/gray in color, or white with black patches.

Photos: 9, 10 & 16

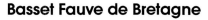

POITEVIN NORMAND
GRIFFON FAUVE DE BRETAGNE
STANDARD GRIFFON VENDEEN

The **Poitevin Normand** is another French hunting hound. Strong and well muscled, this scent hound, now used for larger game, was once a champion hunter of wolves. A dog of great endurance, it can pursue its prey the whole day long.

The **Griffon Fauve de Bretagne** is a dog that is almost unknown outside its French homeland. With its rough, hairy appearance and short legs it is not an elegant dog but it is courageous and easy to manage, and once boldly faced wolves Today it is used to hunt small game and is an excellent pet, good with children, patient and with a kind temperament, if somewhat independent.

The **Standard Griffon Vendéen** is one of the oldest breeds of French hunting hounds, used for small game. A hairy, typically country dog, it is athletic, sturdy and bred for difficult terrain, once used for hunting wolves and wild boar. The smaller types of hounds such as Bassets or Beagles are more common in France but the Standard Griffon Vendéen makes a wonderful pet; very attached to its home and family.

Poitevin Normand

From 60-72cm (23-28 inches) in height and around 35kg (75 pounds) in weight. The coat is short and shiny and may be bi-colored white and orange, or tri-colored (most common) white, orange and black patches.
Photos: 1, 3, 6, 8, 9, 12 & 13

Griffon Fauve de Bretagne

From 47-55cm (18-22 inches) in height and around 20kg (44 pounds) in weight. The coat is medium long, coarse and slightly wavy. Fawn, golden or bright reddish brown in color.
Photos: 2, 4, 5, 11, 15 & 17

Standard Griffon Vendéen

From 60-65cm (23-25 inches) in height and around 35kg (76 pounds) in weight. The coat is medium long and coarse. Fawn, brown and white flecked, white and orange, black and white or tri-colored.
Photos: 7, 10, 14 & 16

GRIFFON BLEU DE GASCOGNE
SMALL GASCONY SAINTONGEAIS
GRIFFON BEAGLE

The **Griffon Bleu de Gascogne** is the rarest of the Gascony Griffons. A great country dog and hunter, the breed is sadly on the verge of extinction.

The **Small Gascony Saintongeais** is a descendant of the Gascony Saintongeais. It has all the requisite instincts of a hunting dog together with speed and a lot of initiative. It is gradually replacing its bigger cousin, now in danger of becoming extinct.

The **Griffon Beagle** is another French dog. Unlike many hounds that hunt in packs, its coat is long and hairy with a full beard. Hardy and speedy, it has all the qualities of the hunting hound but it also likes to be alone or just with its owner, making it an ideal pet. It is a lovely dog with a lively look and attractive expression. Affectionate and with a docile temperament, it won't become neurotic if it does not get three hours exercise a day!

Griffon Bleu de Gascogne
From 42-52cm (16-20 inches) in height. The coat is rough and bluey gray in color with patches.
Photos: 1, 5, 11 & 12

Small Gascony Saintongeais
From 52-60cm (20-23 inches) in height and around 30kg (66 pounds) in weight. The coat is short and dense. White in color with red or black patches and speckles.
Photos: 2, 4, 6 & 8

Griffon Beagle
From 48-55cm (19-21 inches) in height and 15-24kg (33-52 pounds) in weight. The coat is rough and untidy. May be bi-colored fawn and white, or tri-colored fawn, white and one other color.
Photos: 3, 7, 9 & 10

BAVARIAN HOUND
BASSET GRIFFON VENDEEN
GRIFFON NIVERNAIS

The **Bavarian Hound,** or Bavarian Red, as it is also known, is a German dog, related to the Tyrolean Pointer. Used to difficult terrain and high altitudes, it can hunt in any type of country and was even used to hunt the chamois. Today it is used mainly for hare and game birds. Physically it is a robust, muscular dog, resistant to illness. With its gentle temperament it also makes a good pet.

The **Bassett Griffon Vendeen** comes in two sizes: standard and small. The bigger one, being the faster, is used for hunting hare. The smaller one looks more like other Bassets apart from the fringe and general hairiness characteristic of Griffons. A French breed, these dogs are the result of crossing various French and Belgian hunting hounds. Both types make excellent dogs, in a pack or on their own. They also make good pets. A great all-round dog.

The **Griffon Nivernais,** another French breed, is a descendant of the Chien Ségusien and therefore has Oriental antecedents. Today's breed has the blood of many crosses in it including the English Foxhound. A dog which never gives up, it will run all day over any terrain. It is even good in water, but it does not make a successful house pet.

12

15

16

Bavarian Hound

Around 50cm (20 inches) in height and 35kg (76 pounds) in weight. The coat is short and thick and traditionally dark or light red in color, which is why it is also called the Bavarian Red.
Photos: 1, 4, 9, 11 12, 14 & 16

Bassett Griffon Vendéen

From 38-42cm (15-17 inches) in height for the Standard and from 34-38cm (13-15 inches) for the Small type. The coat is rough and hairy and may be one colored sandy or grayish white, or tri-colored and even multi-colored: white, red, orange, bluish gray and sandy.
Photos: 2, 7, 8, 13 & 15

Griffon Nivernais

From 60-68cm (23-26 inches) in height and around 25kg (55 pounds) in weight. The coat is rough, hairy and stands on end, like all Griffons. Gray, grayish blue, black with red patches, and orange and gray in color.
Photos: 3, 5, 6 & 10

13

14

BEAGLE
STANDARD BLEU DE GASCOGNE
ARIEGEOIS

The **Beagle** is an English dog whose origins go back into antiquity. It is mentioned in Chaucer's *Canterbury Tales*. It has a characteristic carrying voice, a beautifully colored coat and an intelligence which makes it one of the most astute hunting breeds. Despite being one of the smallest hounds (Queen Elizabeth the First had a pack of "pocket" Beagles each said to be less than 10 inches high), it will follow large game as happily as small and is fearless and tireless. A favorite dog in the United States where it hunts hare, wild boar, foxes and deer and is also seen on the race track. When not used to hunt, it makes a wonderful pet; playful and very attached to its family.

The **Standard Bleu de Gascogne** comes from Southern France and, as can be seen from its long ears, is probably descended from the Bloodhound. It looks slim and tall on its long legs, with a noble head and sturdy, clean cut limbs. Once a famous hunter of wolves this breed is now becoming more and more rare. Its extremely sensitive nose has made it a great hunter, if not the fastest of pack dogs. Today it is used to hunt deer and hare and prefers to hunt in a pack, where it is at its best.

The **Ariegeois** is unknown to the general public outside its home in Ariege, France. A quality hunting dog used for small and large game, it is elegant and adapts to all types of terrain. Calm, affectionate and with a gentle nature it also makes a good pet.

11

15

12

16

17

13

14

Beagle

From 37-42cm (14-16 inches) in height for the Standard Beagle and from 30-36cm (11-14 inches) for the Small breed. There is no standard weight but the Large Beagle is around 17kg (38 pounds). The coat is short and flat and, ideally, black, white and red in color.

Photos: 2, 3, 7, 14, 15 & 16

Standard Bleu de Gascogne

From 63-70cm (25-27 inches) in height and around 35kg (76 pounds) in weight. Characterized by its bluish gray color and long ears. The coat is short but full. Bluish gray flecks on a white background with black patches give an over all impression that the dog is slate colored or "blue."

Photos: 1, 5, 10, 12 & 17

Ariegeois

From 55-60cm (22-23 inches) in height and 28-30kg (60-66 pounds) in weight. The coat is fine, close cropped and black and white in color, sometimes flecked with blue.

Photos: 4, 6, 8, 9, 11 & 13

DOGS FOR THE HANDICAPPED, RESCUE AND GUARD DOGS

DOGS FOR THE HANDICAPPED

A dog's senses are far superior to ours. They see better, hear better and possess a much better sense of smell and direction than ours. These faculties mean that they can often cope in an environment in which man would find himself at a loss. So the dog can be a great help, both in coming to our rescue when we are in danger and in making up for the handicaps or deficiencies which can afflict humans. A dog which we have always thought of as just a faithful fireside pet may save a child from drowning, rescue a skier buried in an avalanche, be a seeing-eye dog for the blind or go to the aid of a wounded soldier. It may even become a sniffer dog, tracking down drugs, or may carry messages in time of war. Certain breeds are famous for their rescue work: Labradors, Newfoundlands and Saint Bernards for example, but other breeds less known for this ability also do good work, including Boxers, German Shepherds (better known for their police and security work), Dalmatians and, most surprising of all, French poodles. They all do their job conscientiously and are perfectionists.

The Labrador is a very important helper to the mobile handicapped. No breed can beat it at unhooking the

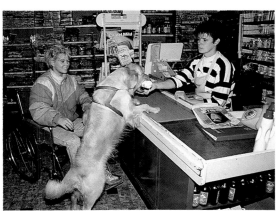

telephone, pulling a wheelchair, opening a door or warning a blind person not to cross the road when a car is coming. With its highly developed sense of communication it will even do the shopping, taking a list to the local store and bringing back what is wanted.

The seeing-eye dog is a well known helper in today's society, but less well known is the trained dog for those who have difficulty in hearing. In the United States and in Great Britain dogs are now being trained to act as their owner's ears: they go to the door when the bell rings, increase the speed of their walk when they hear an ambulance coming, show their owner (by nudging or other action) if a noise suggests danger and bring the phone when it rings. They can even let their owner know if the baby is crying or pick up a pair of fallen spectacles. And it is not just pedigree dogs that make good hearing dogs or helpers for the handicapped. Some of the most successful and professional at their job are mongrels.

Dogs for the handicapped undergo special and rigorous training and are chosen for their qualities of gentleness, patience, flexibility in learning and obedience. These precious animals give their owners back the joy of living and may truly be called "man's best friend."

MOUNTAIN RESCUE DOGS

Avalanche rescue dogs are capable of working for 15 or 16 hours without a break.

The **Saint Bernard**, with the Red Cross band on its forehead, is one of the symbols of Switzerland. The Barry (its name in German dialect, meaning "bear") has been associated with the Hospice du Saint Bernard for more than two centuries, during which time it has saved countless lives. The American Saint Bernard Club was one of the first breed societies in the United States. With a highly developed sense of smell, great resistance to fatigue and bad weather conditions, it is a very intelligent dog and was, until recent decades, the king of mountain rescue breeds. It is capable of finding a man buried under many feet of snow and of spotting him from 50 yards away.

Side by side with such giants as the Saint Bernard and the **German Shepherd,** it is fun to see the little **Scottish Terrier** (which once hunted rats down the Scottish mines), searching out and rescuing avalanche victims.

ARMY DOGS

The star performer of the armed forces' dogs is, of course, the **German Shepherd,** which undergoes rigorous training designed to make it the top professional dog, with a multiplicity of skills. From a very young age the army dog is trained in obedience, security and rescue work and will be able to detect mines, guard ammunition depots, go on patrol and on the ski slopes, and rescue avalanche victims, as well as acting as a messenger if required.

The **Canaan Dog** is a fairly unknown breed outside Israel, where during recent troubled times it has often and very successfully been used as a liaison dog, carrying messages. It is also a good seeing-eye dog, active, intelligent, sweet natured and easy to train. It is able to master many skills and, like the German Shepherd and the Labrador Retriever, is useful for rescue operations at sea or in any water.

DOGS USED IN DISASTERS AND TO SNIFF OUT DRUGS

Wherever there is a disaster the **German Shepherd** will be found: at earthquakes, explosions, urban gas leaks, etc. This breed, like the **Boxer**, is able to search out victims, inform its handler, dig out people from cooled lava or thick mud, bark in warning that a victim is buried under rubble, alert the first rescue services on the scene; and all of this even in the middle of night. An unexpected dog to find doing this work is the **French Poodle**. Normally to be seen petted and cossetted in the show ring, or in a lady's living room, it is just as successful a rescue dog as its bigger friends. The highly developed sense of smell in dogs is extremely useful in this work.

Certain breeds, including **German Shepherds, Belgian Shepherds, Labrador Retrievers** and **Golden Retrievers,** are used to detect drugs. These dogs work in airports, railroad and bus stations and all passenger transport areas which are international ports of entry. They make an inseparable team with their police handlers and are trained in special centers from which they graduate with their lifetime human partner. From time to time handler and dog may take a refresher course to make sure they are always operationally perfect and to catch up with new techniques or new drug research. A Labrador Retriever takes two months to complete the sniffer dog course for Hashish and Marijuana, and there is fierce competition for handler and dog teams to win the training awards.

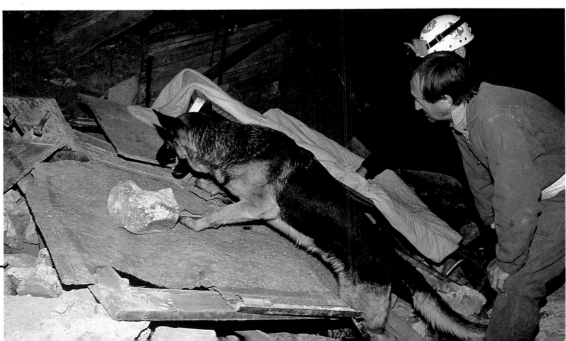

SEA RESCUE DOGS

The **Newfoundland** has practically the monopoly when it comes to rescuing people from the water. Its robust, hardy build, remarkable initiative and calmness make it the perfect dog for working in the water. Some are so used to rescuing drowning victims that they won't even let their owner take a swim without leaping in and pulling them out! These qualities are inherent in the breed, but even the Newfoundland has to go through a regular obedience and training course to be efficient. On graduating the Newfoundland is able to find persons in difficulty even in a high sea and bring them back to shore. They are able to jump from boats to fish someone out and they learn to rescue them by pulling the person to dry land by the arm. They also learn to perform rescue operations in the fastest possible time and by the shortest route. This dog, a rescuer by instinct, is as courageous and faithful a friend to humans when all is well, as it is when danger threatens.

The **Labrador Retriever** is a worthy second to the Newfoundland when it comes to rescuing people from the water. Legend has it that this dog, with its soft, smooth coat had an otter for its ancestor. Is that why it is such a good swimmer? It, too, comes from Newfoundland and is quite at home in extremely cold waters. Its intelligence, determination and legacy of once being a retriever of fish for cod fishermen makes the Labrador Retriever a much appreciated helper at scenes of rescue at sea. Its otter-like tail and slight webbing between its toes are an advantage in the water.

AMUSING DOGS

It is said that the dog is the closest animal to humans and that it makes us laugh more than any other. Some dogs are amusing simply because of their appearance. The Chinese Hairless dog, for instance, with the strange tuft of hair on its head and naked body, or the Shar-Pei, buried in great folds of skin, are both naturally funny. Some mongrels, perhaps half Labrador Retriever half heaven knows what, can be very amusing to look at. But the more a dog makes us laugh the more we love it. After all, a mongrel is unique; it is almost impossible to find two the same!

We also find the dog's ability to copy the actions of humans amusing: it can carry the newspaper, get car sick, lean out of a window or open a door. And emotionally, too, they imitate us: they can get in a bad mood and sulk; they can give you a melting look; be playful, irritating and as annoying to their masters or mistresses as small children can be to their parents. Irresistibly lovable at times when they look their worst; getting out of the water for instance, wet, bedraggled and miserable and having lost all their panache and nobility.

Dogs tolerate being dressed up and will happily join in the fun. See the dog over the page wearing his homemade crown, or the sheepdog, above left, wearing glasses and the hunting dog, left, with shoes on.

Man and dog copy each other: the dog pretends to be human with his owner and the owner begins to look like his dog; a strange phenomenon which has been pointed out a million times in movies and television shows from Walt Disney onward. And we find this irresistibly funny. Sometimes it is the way we dress our dogs that makes them amusing: in a winter coat or with a ribbon in the top knot of a toy dog. It is difficult not to be amused by the strutting animals who, nose in air, walk along as though they were humans showing off their new wardrobe.

But we also have to ask ourselves "Is there some mystery about the dog which we do not understand?" Perhaps we find it safest to be amused by them.

INDEX

INDEX

127

PICTURE CREDITS

The majority of the illustrations in this book have been drawn from the files of the Cogis picture agency, and were taken by the following photographers: Ann Amblin, Jérôme Hutin, Jean-Michel Labat, Gérard Lacz, Yves Lanceau, Stéphane Lefebvre-Juvet, Sylvie Lepage, François Nicaise, Gérald Pottier, D and S Simon, Danièle Taulin-Mommel, François Varin, Serge Vedie, Frank Vidal.
All other illustrations as follows: R Benali 59; S Phillipot 60 (2); M Peccoux 62 (3), 121 (17); Réglain 62 (10); Monnestier 92-93; Kermani/Liaison 11 (10, 11 & 13); Charles/Liaison 111 (2); Breese/Liaison 114 (2); Shone 115 (9 & 12); L. Sola 115 (13 & 14); Liaison 120 (1); Weiner 120 (4); Benainous 121 (18); Manfred 121 (19); Abacus 124 (3); F Apesteguy 124/125 (12); R. Gaillarde 124 (6); Sennet/Liaison 124 (10); B de Hogues 124 (15).

Produced by Copyright Studio, Paris
Design: Nicole Leymarie
Layout: Natalie Boibessot
Picture Research: Veronique Cardineau
with the kind assistance of Pascale Renambot of the Cogis agency
Translated from the French by Carole Fahy
for Bookdeals Translations, PO Box 263, Taunton, Somerset